HOMETOWN TALES is a series of books pairing exciting new voices with some of the most talented and important authors at work today. Each of the writers has contributed an original tale on the theme of hometown, exploring places and communities in the UK where they have lived or think of as home.

Some of the tales are fiction and some are narrative non-fiction – they are all powerful, fascinating and moving, and aim to celebrate regional diversity and explore the meaning of home.

HOMETOWN TALES
MIDLANDS

KERRY YOUNG
CAROLYN SANDERSON

WEIDENFELD & NICOLSON

First published in Great Britain in 2018 by Weidenfeld & Nicolson
an imprint of The Orion Publishing Group Ltd
Carmelite House, 50 Victoria Embankment
London EC4Y 0DZ

An Hachette UK Company

1 3 5 7 9 10 8 6 4 2

Home Is Where the Heart Is © Kerry Young 2018
Times and Seasons © Carolyn Sanderson 2018

The moral right of Kerry Young and Carolyn Sanderson to be identified
as the authors of this work has been asserted in accordance
with the Copyright, Designs and Patents Act of 1988.

A CIP catalogue record for this book is available from the British Library.

ISBN (Hardback) 978 1 4746 0803 9
ISBN (eBook) 978 1 4746 0804 6

Typeset at The Spartan Press Ltd,
Lymington, Hants

Printed and bound in Great Britain by Clays Ltd, Elcograf S.p.A

www.orionbooks.co.uk

CONTENTS

Home Is Where the Heart Is

Kerry Young

KERRY YOUNG was born in Kingston, Jamaica, and moved to England in 1965. She is the author of three novels, all available from Bloomsbury: *Pao*, shortlisted for the Costa First Novel Award and the Commonwealth Book Prize; *Gloria*, which was longlisted for the OCM Bocas Prize for Caribbean Literature and nominated for the International IMPAC Dublin Literary Award; and *Show Me A Mountain*.

Kerry is a reader for The Literary Consultancy, a tutor for the Arvon Foundation, and a Royal Literary Fund Fellow. She is also Honorary Assistant Professor in the School of English at the University of Nottingham and Honorary Creative Writing Fellow at the University of Leicester.

kerryyoung.co.uk
@KerryYoungWrite

SOMETHING HAPPENED. LONG before I got here. In this place they call a cul-de-sac. In the house across the street. Where Mr Eric and Miss Betsy live. Although, at first I wasn't sure if it was Eric or Ernie because Aunt Edith called him both. Like she was talking about Morecambe and Wise. After watching them on the television in *Two of a Kind*. Miss Betsy is definitely Betsy though. Not Bessie like the Bessie Smith I used to listen to. No, I've never heard any blues music coming out of that house. Blues was for back then. When I spent time with my father. The Blues. That was all he cared about.

Not like Sister Margaret making us listen to the Rediffusion because she wanted us to hear proper English voices speaking proper English the proper way and playing proper music appropriate for proper young ladies. Like us. That is what Sister

Margaret said. She didn't want our ears bruised by any free-spirited Jamaican radio station playing calypso and ska, and other kinds of riff-raff rhythms. The sort of thing that surrounded you any time you set foot outside of the house. Not that she let us go into town that much. And never alone. In case the devil got a hold of us, or worse, somebody we knew come to take us back to the life she had saved us from in the first place. It was protection. That is what she was doing. Protecting us girls from the terrible lives we had already known.

No blues. In fact, no music coming from that house whatsoever. Eric/Ernie and Betsy. Him, a policeman before he retired. That is what they say. So all day, every day, the two of them are shut up together in that house they call a bungalow. Number 14, James Street, Fleckney. Named after the king, like all of the streets around this corner of the village. Named after English kings and queens – Victoria, Elizabeth, Edward, Albert and James. And Gladstone Street, even though he wasn't a king. But it is from my bedroom window in number 24, James Street, that I can see Eric/Ernie and Betsy's curtains opening and closing. Because I have the front room and Aunt Edith and Uncle Harold have the back room so they can look over the wheat fields behind the house while I look over the road.

And what I see is Eric/Ernie's orange and white hanging baskets and their neat little front yard. Except it is called a garden. With some oblong grass and a narrow bed that edges all the way around it planted with small flowers. Little yellow things and some pink and blue. Things that don't grow any taller than a foot. If that. Not like a hibiscus bush or a poinsettia. Not like a beautiful purple bougainvillea climbing up the wall. Or even something to give them some food. Like an ackee tree or breadfruit or avocado. Or a nice red flamboyant for the decoration. No. Nothing like that. Just these tiny little nothing flowers that make you wonder why he bothers with them at all. Labouring all hours from morning until night. Every livelong day for the last two months I have been watching him. Since coming here from Jamaica, on the BOAC airplane with Sister Margaret. And Dr Morrison. And little John. June 1967.

They are tidy though, his flowers. But that is about all you can say about them. Uncle Harold says Eric/Ernie has a big back garden too, which I guess is also some oblong grass edged with neat little flowers of no particular significance whatsoever. But who am I to judge? I am only twelve years old and a foreigner.

Next to Eric/Ernie and Betsy is the family that Uncle Harold doesn't like. He calls them layabouts because none of them go to work. Mother and father and three grown boys. And not a single day's work between them. That is what he said. Uncle Harold.

'You see that?' he said to me, pointing to the blue Ford Zephyr parked in their driveway. 'That is the result of a welfare state that can't tell need from greed.'

I raised my eyebrows and looked up at him. Because he is a tall man. Uncle Harold. And broad across the shoulders.

'Five grown people who should be contributing to the economy of this country. Five people who could be lending a hand to make this a better place for all. Who could be helping to build something. Who could be making Britain great. But no, all they do instead is draw the dole each Thursday and park broken-down jalopies out front.'

'For the whole world to see and suffer?' I asked. I've heard him say it before.

'Never a truer word said.' He nudged his chin in the direction of number 16. 'Too comfortable to even bother raising a little finger. Lazy scroungers who would rather wallow in the gutter while still thinking they are better than you.'

I don't know if they are in the gutter. I don't know if they think they are better than me. I don't know if they have need or greed. All I know is that their house is *council* and Uncle Harold has opinions about them. Like he does about most things. Keep your room tidy and put things away where they belong. Always wash your hands before you come to the table. Fold the towels neatly in the bathroom and hang them so they can air and dry. Wear your slippers in the house. When you are asked to do something, get up and do it immediately. No ifs or buts or maybes. No later or tomorrow. No question and answer. You get up that instant and do it. Army style. And I do so, exactly as he says, with grace and a good heart, because it is with grace and a good heart that Uncle Harold and Aunt Edith have let me come to this country and live with them. And it is with grace and a good heart that God Almighty put us on this earth to see if we can turn our backs on the sins that call to us each and every minute of the day. Sister Margaret says.

Sister Margaret is a Presbyterian. That is how she knows Aunt Edith. From when they were children going to church together in Edinburgh. Not that Aunt Edith goes to church now because the only related Presbyterian is a United Reformed in Leicester and that isn't the same thing at all. And much too far to travel. According to her. So, sometimes she goes to the Baptist in the village. Better a church completely unrelated than some kind of distant cousin. I think that is the way she sees it. And at least she can walk to the Baptist. Not like trying to catch a Sunday service bus to the city. And back. Anyway, she says God won't mind where she's bending her knees as long as she does right by Him every day of the week.

Uncle Harold is not Presbyterian. He is British Army. Or used to be. Somehow he ended up in Edinburgh and somehow met Aunt Edith. They somehow got married. And she somehow moved back here with him. To Leicestershire. Years ago. That is how she told it to me. With a lot of somehows, and I reckoned if that was a good enough explanation for her, then it was good enough for me. Uncle Harold used to drum in the army. In the marching band. But he doesn't do that any more. There is nowhere in this semi-detached house for him to be playing any drums. Not a snare, never mind a full kit. So, instead, he works at the Premier Drums factory in Wigston and just taps with his 7A sticks around the house, which are really too short and light for him. But Aunt Edith wouldn't be happy with a pair of 5B or 2B sticks crashing into the furniture. Anyway, he knows he has missed his chance to be Gene Krupa or Buddy Rich. So he says.

They are good people. That is what Sister Margaret said when she told me we were coming to England.

'The only way you are going to get away from him is to leave this island. Do you understand?'

Yes, I did. I understood, because no matter how much Sister Margaret told him to stay away from the house he still kept coming over and causing all sorts of trouble and arguments that nobody could put a stop to. Not Sister Margaret or Gloria or Hyacinth. Not even the police that one of the girls would sometimes run to fetch. Not even them, because he was my father and I was his child and he could come and take me away from Sister Margaret any time he wanted. Which is what he did, every so often, when his house needed a good clean or if he had a mind to make some extra money from the friends he invited over to do to me the things men do. And then, when he was done feeling like he wanted to bother feeding me, he would bring me back to Sister Margaret worse for wear.

*

Next door to Family Need and Greed – in the other half of the semi-detached, which is a new idea to me, houses joined together like that – lives the tall, thin man. All on his own. A sad example of a man who wears nothing but brown. That is such a sorrowful colour. Every day. And a not-so-crisp, soft-looking white shirt. He has a big bald head, over which he carefully brushes a long strand of hair. Like it can cover anything. Aunt Edith says he has a job at the council. In the planning department. And every morning at 7:15 he closes his green front door gingerly, pushes against it three times to make sure it is shut, walks down his path, opens and shuts his low, rusty, iron gate and makes his way to the bus stop at the bottom of Gladstone Street. I know that, not because I have ever followed him, but because that is the only bus stop at this end of the village. To catch the bus to Leicester. To the council offices where he works. That is all there is. Apart from his faded wooden fence and path of grey paving slabs.

'Who is that man, Aunt Edith?'

'Don't you concern yourself with that. If the Good Lord wanted you to know He would have issued you an invitation to tea at number 18.'

At number 20, turning the corner of the cul-de-sac,

nearly out of my sight but not quite, lives Him/Her. Meek and humble. That is how the house feels. Even though there is always a strong pulse coming from it. Like a heartbeat, or warm, moist breath. Regular and constant. But He/She is never seen. And no one ever goes to the house. Except Mr Roberts, the greengrocer, who every Friday morning leaves a full box on the back doorstep. At 11.30 precisely. And Mr Gaskell from the Co-op at 12 noon. And Brian, the milkman, who leaves one pint of gold top at the back door every day except Sundays. Because on Saturdays he leaves two. And the only person who ever goes to that front door is the paper boy. In the early hours of each morning. To slide a broadsheet into the letter box. Halfway in and halfway out. And, if it's raining, the newspaper is wrapped in a light blue plastic bag to protect it against the weather. There is the postman of course, who calls from time to time. And even takes letters away with him to post, even though I know that isn't really allowed. Who is writing to Him/Her anyway? And how does He/She live like that? Doesn't He/She ever feel the need for a little fresh air?

'Do you know why He/She lives like that, Aunt Edith?'

'Mine is not to question why. Or who or when or where.'

I don't understand what she means. Does she know or not?

'And yours is not to do any of those things either. Yours is to mind your own business and know that in a few short weeks, school is going to commence. And you will be catching the bus to join the other children as you all put your attention to learning something to make your futures.'

That, I understand. After all, it is the reason Sister Margaret brought me here. To make my future. Just like the man in the street said to me. The one from Aunt Edith's church.

'Come to make a better life, have you?' And then, shifting his heavy shopping bag from one hand to the next, he said, 'Streets aren't paved with gold, you know. Not like they told you. You have to work to cleanse your black soul.' Who says that sort of thing to a child? Or an adult come to that. Aunt Edith said he was just making conversation. Passing the time of day because he didn't know what to say to me. Perhaps he should have just said 'Hello. How are you?' But funnily enough, the same thing happened one day when Aunt Edith was buying some spools of thread. In fact, the lady came from right behind the counter to feel my hair and give it a tug.

'You will need to keep that tidy when you start school.'

How did it come to be that everybody a) knew all about my situation and b) thought it was all right to say whatever they wanted to me? Especially, 'You people come here thinking the streets are paved with gold.' There goes that phrase again. But then she followed it with, 'But there are no handouts in this life. No free lunches. You have to work. Earn your living. Put a roof over your head. Not just sit down and think anybody owes you anything. This country was made from hard work, sweat and tears.' Now she is picking up the yellow, green, red and black embroidery colours Aunt Edith asked for. Counting them into the bag and folding over the top several times, she says, 'Free schooling, so you get a good education. Free doctors so you stay healthy. And the generosity of Edith and Harold who are putting a roof over your head and clothes on your back and food in your stomach.' She holds up the brown paper bag. 'I bet you didn't have any of that where you come from.' She doesn't need an answer to her question.

'I hope you are grateful. That is all I have to say. Grateful like you should be.'

I look up at Aunt Edith who is standing there neutral. Clutching her wicker shopping basket. I can see she is ready to leave. She isn't liking this conversation any more than I am. She just doesn't know what to say. Village life is small. There is only one grocery store. One greengrocer. One doctor. One district nurse. There is one junior school, where Aunt Edith works two mornings a week helping the school secretary in the office. One post office that will also cash cheques. One newsagent. One corner shop with an off-licence that is open later at night and on a Sunday when the Co-op is closed. One public house. Not that Aunt Edith ever goes in there. One butchers, which she does visit. One family bakery for home-made loaves and cakes. One small taxi company. Well, one taxi actually. Life is difficult if you fall out with these people. I can understand that.

'Anyway,' Aunt Edith says as we walk back to James Street, 'it's just talk. They don't mean anything by it. Even when I first came here they would say all sorts of things about the Scottish. Right to my face. While I was standing in their shop, buying their goods and passing over the money. It was a joke to them.'

She laughs. But it's a tense one that sticks in her throat. Like the day in the post office when she was surprised at the cost of the stamp. 'Sixpence? Really?' she said while searching in her purse for the change. And a woman in the queue behind us said, 'Try taking it there yourself for less.'

'Just a joke,' Aunt Edith said afterwards. Except she didn't laugh, the woman, when she said it. She wasn't even smiling. I know because I turned to look at her.

'It didn't seem like a joke to me.'

'You will get used to it.'

There is a lot to get used to. First of all, everything is called something else. Potato chips are crisps. Cookies are biscuits. Lunch is dinner. The trunk of the car is the boot. You walk on the pavement. The Band-Aid is a plaster. A store is a shop. A truck is a lorry. Plus, everything looks different. The houses are small and closed in with low ceilings and tiny rooms, especially the terraces that are joined together in long blocks with a different family behind each and every door. Detached, semi, bungalow, flat, maisonette. Red brick everywhere. That is what England looks like. Red brick. The fields are wide and open. But they are huge and empty. Not like a cane field or banana plantation with body and height. These fields are thin and spiritless, abandoned and forsaken, even while the crops are growing in them. And the place is barren. If you needed a piece of wood or a length of string or a twist of wire to do a small job, you wouldn't be able to find it. You can't go out back or under the house for anything, because there is nothing there.

Potatoes, potatoes and more potatoes. Grilled pork chops. Boiled ham. Stewed beef. Roast chicken on Sunday. Cabbage and carrots cooked beyond recognition. And none of it with any seasoning or taste whatsoever. The gravy sometimes has flavour but that comes from a packet, so it's the same every time. Not a grain of rice in sight. No rice and peas or fried plantain. Green bananas, yams, ackee and salt-fish, sweet potato pudding. No pineapple or mango or sweet sop or guava or june plum or jackfruit. But I am still grateful.

Grateful for the absence of worry and anxiety. Knowing that each day will be followed by the next. In this house. With these people who have committed themselves to caring for me. That was what Aunt Edith said to Sister Margaret and Dr Morrison as she and Uncle Harold sat drinking tea with them in the front room.

'Well, Edith, this is the end of a very long journey.'

'And the beginning of another, Margaret. I am so grateful that you thought to write to me and offer us this wonderful opportunity.' She gently stroked the back of Uncle Harold's hand.

Sister Margaret smiled. 'The adoption papers are all here. Signed and sealed.' She leant forward and lightly tapped the large brown envelope she had placed on the coffee table.

'I don't know how to thank you.'

'What you are doing is thanks enough: giving a home to a child who needs one. And you can rest assured all is in perfect order.' Sister Margaret opened the envelope and flicked through the pages. 'The child's father has signed right here.' She pointed to the spot on the page. 'So, you see all is well. Our rewards are on earth as well as in heaven.'

And that was when Aunt Edith said it. 'Harold and I commit ourselves to caring for her with every ounce of effort and every breath we take.' Nobody had ever said anything like that about me before. Never. It made me cry, silently. Eavesdropping as I was from the hallway. And especially with the silence that had fallen across the front room.

And then Aunt Edith said, 'You and George are visiting family?'

'Yes, and enrolling John into school in Edinburgh. He's five years old now.'

'So, you came for the trip, Dr Morrison?'

'Actually, we are staying,' he said, a little down in the mouth.

And that was it. That was how Sister Margaret took me from her home for young mothers and brought me to England. Having gifted my baby to the Catholic nuns at the orphanage. And having bought me from my father. With hard cash. That is how I ended up at 24 James Street staring out at Eric/Ernie and Betsy. And at number 22: old Mrs Glover with the walking stick and her lodgers, Joan and Stewart. And next door to us, on the other side, at number 26: Stella who was about the same age as me and lived with her mum and dad, Mr and Mrs Sullivan.

What I thought about as I watched the car drive away was how thoughtful Sister Margaret was to have brought a wide-toothed comb and moisturiser with her, and taken the time to show Aunt Edith how to plait my hair. And how nice it was that she told Aunt Edith she would write. And how warm and soft her body felt when she hugged me goodbye. I wondered how my baby was doing with the nuns. And if Gloria and Hyacinth and the other girls would miss me as much as I was going to miss them. And if my father would have any regrets after he finished spending Sister Margaret's money. And if he would care about having lost a daughter, or even remember that he had a grandson.

Aunt Edith says we have to get the school uniform. From the school outfitters in Leicester. So we walk to Gladstone Street and get on the County Travel coach. It is green and cream with comfortable seats, and no upstairs or open access at the back. Not like the brown corporation buses in the city. This bus is just on one level with the driver taking the fares. No conductor. And it's not packed and sweaty like a Kingston bus. It's calm and empty like the sleepy villages we pass through, and the meadows in Wistow Park with the sheep and cattle grids.

It takes almost an hour before the bus comes to its final stop in Northampton Square. Opposite the police station. We cross the road and walk down Granby Street, past the hotel and left into Belvoir Street. Except it is called 'Beaver'. And then we turn left again into Stamford Street and climb the four concrete steps to enter this emporium that sells the uniforms for every school in Leicestershire. Skirts and trousers, blouses, shirts and blazers, striped ties in every colour and combination. I need two charcoal-grey skirts, five white shirts, one green-and-yellow striped tie and a bottle-green blazer with a school badge that Aunt Edith will have to sew on to the breast pocket. But even though I think the gabardine fabric is nicer, Aunt Edith says I will have the woolly blazer. It feels itchy. But it is cheaper, so I don't complain. I am grateful. I am safe. No one is forcing me to do unsavoury things or beating me when I refuse to do it. The woolly blazer is fine.

The skirt is too long. It will need shortening. That is what Aunt Edith says. The lady in the store says, 'The length is determined by the waist measurement, madam.' Which means what? Is she saying I am too short? No. She is saying I am too fat. But that, I have noticed, is how the English speak. In a roundabout way, so you can't understand what they mean. You have to try to work it out. Like, in the store, Aunt Edith might ask, 'Do you have any Reckitt's blue bags?' And the attendant might answer, 'Someone else was asking me about that this morning.' Which is not the answer to the question. There is a lot of guesswork involved in talking with English people.

The other thing is how detached people are. Like, here we are in the city, Leicester, where everybody is just going about their business like each other don't exist. Like they are walking the street all on their own, strolling right past you without even looking your way to exchange a hello or good day. It seems cold and unfriendly not even to give a nod of recognition. Just to say, yes, I know you are there. In Jamaica, strangers are not strangers. People make contact with each other. They greet you. Whap'am bredda. Whap'am sista. Wah gwaan? And they make observations. Like someone might say, 'Yu face is nice,' or 'Yu hair is nice.' Or in my case, 'You are a fleshy girl.' There is nothing rude or nasty about that. It is just an observation, an acknowledgement that you are there. They have noticed you. Someone might even come up to you and squeeze your arm and say, 'How come yu look so strong?' It is human contact. It has directness about it. And it is true. I am chubby and I do look strong. I know that. And my face is nice. Aunt Edith says.

Two white Aertex blouses and a short green skirt with thick pants for games, and we are done. Woolworths for a school satchel, pencils and pens and the wicker basket I will need to carry the ingredients for cookery class. The fabric stall on the market for the length of grey and yellow gingham I will take to the needlework class to sew the apron I need for cookery. Clarks for shoes. Marks and Spencer for pants, called knickers, vests and socks and, finally, a visit to Brucciani because Aunt Edith is 'parched' and needs a cup of tea. We have ham salad sandwiches and I have a Coca-Cola float. Except it wasn't Coca-Cola, it was just cola. So the waitress said. With vanilla ice cream on top.

A week later, on the morning of 25 September, I was dressed and ready, with the brown leather satchel on my shoulder. Feeling spick and span and very grown-up in my jacket and tie, as Aunt Edith and I took the bus to school. She said we had to report to the headmaster's office, so we asked the first adult we came across, a thin lady with glasses who was directing the traffic of children in the school playground.

'Up to the top of the yard, through the double doors and you'll be opposite the hall. Turn left along the corridor. Take the first right, passing the hall again on your right, and keep going until you pass the library on your left and carry on straight up to the headmaster's office.'

He was short. That was the first thing I noticed when he got up from behind his big oak desk. Short and somewhat squat. Not fat exactly. But with puffy hands, one of which he reached out to Aunt Edith.

'Welcome, welcome. I am Mr Hollingsworth. Please, do sit down.' He pointed to the two green-cushioned straight-back chairs facing his desk. We sat while he walked around and reseated himself. 'We are very pleased to be welcoming you to the school.' He looked at Aunt Edith. 'She has already missed the first year of high school, as you know, but everything is salvageable.' He smiled. 'I have read all of the information you included in your letter of application, Mrs Jenson, but is there anything else you would like to tell me? Or ask?'

'No, nothing. I think I covered everything in the letter and the information I received from the school was very thorough.'

'Perfect.' He rubbed his chubby hands together. 'Children come to us from their junior school. That is how things normally happen. In this case, things have happened a little differently. So we don't have any idea about you.' He looked over at me. 'No test results for reading or writing or arithmetic.' He paused. 'Or anything else for that matter.'

I could see children moving around through the leaded window behind him, while next to me, Aunt Edith fiddled with the rim of the hat she had resting in her lap. A soft felt hat. Grey with a knitted pink rose on the side.

'So what I propose is that we spend the day doing a few basic tests so we can see where things are up to.' He looked directly at me for the first time. And staring at him like that, I noticed that Mr Hollingsworth had hair growing out of his nose. And his ears. Not great long strands of hair, just little strays. Although the ones poking out of his ears were more like bits of fluff – little balls of grey fluff, which was funny because the hair on his head was brown.

'So that's it.' He clapped his hands. Twice. 'By the end of the day, we'll know which class to put you in. Which stream will best meet your needs.' He swallowed. 'Does that make sense?'

Aunt Edith said it did and asked him what he wanted her to do.

'That is entirely up to you, Mrs Jenson. But this young lady will be busy for quite some time. Certainly for the rest of the morning, and then in the afternoon we'll have someone show her around the school. It will be a full day.'

'So not worth me waiting for her then?'

'Entirely up to you, as I said. We can make you comfortable in the staff room if you wish or, if you prefer, you can go away and come back around three-thirty. Otherwise we will put her on the school bus to Fleckney at the end of the day. Entirely up to you.'

Aunt Edith decided to leave, but not before asking me several times if I would be all right. I didn't want her to go, but I said I would be OK so she kissed me on the cheek and left, looking as sad and confused as I felt inside. I saw the top of her hat a few moments later. Going up the road to the bus stop. And her hand rising with a small cotton handkerchief to mop her face.

The school secretary, Mrs Watts, sat me down at a small wooden desk specially put into the corner of her office so that she could keep an eye on me. That is what she told me. Not in a threatening way, but in a kindly sort of way, like she was looking after me. She gave me a fresh writing pad and two pencils. I told her I had pen and pencils. And a rubber and ruler. She smiled. Her teeth were a little crooked. And very small. Like thin knitting needles sticking out of her gums.

'Well then, seems you have everything you need.'

She smiled again and shuffled away on her very flat shoes, which were more like slippers. My eyes followed her towards her desk, at the side of which was a large shopping bag with a pair of black shoes peeking out. Court shoes with modest heels. That is what Sister Margaret would have called them.

'I wear them on the bus. To and from school.' She jutted out her chin at the shoes. And then looking down at her feet, 'These are more comfortable for all day.' Answering me like I had asked, which I hadn't.

'Which would you prefer first? General knowledge, reading and comprehension, English or mathematics?'

I chose mathematics, which involved a lot of addition, subtraction, division and multiplication as well as calculations about how many apples John had if he had twenty per cent of five dozen, or if Jane caught the bus at 8.30 and the journey took ninety-eight minutes, what time would she arrive? Page after page of sums that Mrs Watts said should take me an hour and which she timed. I was comfortable. Content. I was good at arithmetic. That is why I had chosen to do that test first. And I finished a good while before Mrs Watts told me to put down my pencil.

For English, I had a lot of grammar questions to answer, and word quizzes and a crossword. Sentences

I had to complete by choosing the correct word from a list, making paragraphs from jumbled-up sentences, crisscrossing my pencil to make as many words as possible from the letters in the squares. And writing each of them down neatly in the boxes provided. For comprehension, I had to read a story about two children going on holiday with their mother and father, the things they packed and the cottage they stayed in, and how nice the garden was, and how kind the parents were, loving the children and playing with them, and how they all ran along the seashore with the dog called Woof. And then I had to answer some questions. So far, so good. Sister Margaret and her proper English lessons had prepared me well. But the next part was a shock. Write a short composition about a holiday I had been on with my parents. What was I to write? I had never been on holiday with my parents. I didn't even know what a holiday was. Not really. Who goes on *holiday* in Jamaica? I fumbled and had nothing to say. I couldn't even make something up because I had no idea what to imagine.

What happened next was worse. General knowledge. I couldn't name any of the trees or birds or flowers, except the rose because I'd seen that in one of Sister Margaret's picture books. There were no orchids, or bird of paradise, or oleander. No crepe myrtle or frangipani or hummingbird to point out. I knew nothing of the outlaws in Sherwood Forest or who wrote the plays they performed in the Globe, which I thought was a round representation of the world that spun on an axis in Sister Margaret's schoolroom. I didn't know anything about Miss Potter's rabbit, or who Peter Pan's enemy was, or what adventures Alice had in Wonderland. I didn't even know who was the Prime Minister of England in World War Two. Nothing about the Romans or sinking passenger liners or how many wives King Henry had, never mind their names. Or what happened in London in September 1666. So I guessed I would fail that part.

Finally, I had to read to Mrs Watts. A story about a girl who spent all of her time in the house doing chores with her mother while her brother was outside having fun with his dad. Her life seemed very sad and I was sad because I knew I hadn't pronounced all the words exactly the way Mrs Watts wanted me to. Not said them in the proper English way. How I knew? Because she kept asking me to repeat myself, like she didn't understand what I was saying. She smiled at me anyway, when I had finished, and told me to pack up my things because Peter was coming to take me to lunch. I felt quite downhearted at the end.

Peter Hollingsworth is the headmaster's son. He is in the second year like I am going to be. He has wild, bushy hair, not like his father whose hair is short and trimmed. And he talks a lot, because Peter is excited about everything.

In the dining hall, you have to get into a queue with a brown plastic tray. Then you move along following the child in front and you choose what you want to eat, which the dinner lady, Peter said, serves up for you. I chose boiled potatoes with beef stew and cobbler. It reminded me of Jamaican beef soup, without the pumpkin. It even had a sort of floury thing on top that could have been a dumpling. For dessert, I had semolina with a chocolate haystack. That's what Peter called it. It was nice, even though it was so hard that it shattered when I pressed my spoon into it and sent the milk pudding splashing out of the bowl onto the table. Peter said it was OK. It happens all the time. And he got a cloth to mop up the mess. The dinner lady even smiled at him as she passed the rag over the counter. At Sister Margaret's we always had to make our own lunch and saw to the dishes ourselves.

Afterwards, Peter showed me around. Inside the

double doors and turn right at the hall, down the long corridor to the classrooms for history, geography and maths, and on the other side, English and French. Because the teachers stay in their rooms and the children go to them at the beginning of each period. So, there is a lot of walking about. Not like sitting in that one room, all of us girls together, without moving a single inch, with Gloria and Hyacinth and sometimes a Sister from Alpha to help with special subjects. In the main building is also the gym and at the far end the changing rooms for games.

'What games do you do?'

'Well, you have gym of course. Everybody does that. And then girls do hockey in the winter and netball in the summer.'

'I don't know what these things are.'

'You'll learn. Boys play rugby and cricket.'

'I know about cricket.'

Then he showed me the domestic science and needlework rooms. 'We don't go in there because boys do metalwork and woodwork.' And then he waved his arm in the air, to show me where the school buses line up at the end of the day. 'So make sure you get on the right bus. Saddington and Fleckney. It will say it on a piece of cardboard propped up in the front window.'

And then we walked again, across the playground to the biology lab, physics lab and, beyond that, chemistry. I'd never seen anything like this before. The long benches with their gas taps, fume cupboards, tripods, Bunsen burners, glass beakers of varying sizes, bottles with chemicals, the gigantic periodic table of elements fixed to the wall. Peter laughed.

'You'll get used to it.'

A teacher shouted out from the prep room. 'Hello, Peter.'

'New girl, sir.' He took me by the shoulders and turned me towards the door to give sir a good look at me.

'So I see.'

And then Peter spun me around again and we walked out.

'So, what do you think?'

'Of the school?'

'What else?'

'Seems OK.'

'OK? Is that all you have to say? What kind of talk is that anyway? OK. American?'

'Jamaican.'

'Jamaican!' He laughed.

'What do you say then? The English.'

Peter thought about it and then he said, 'Jolly decent, old chap.' And threw his head back and laughed. And his hair bobbled in the sunshine like a slightly tarnished golden halo.

We still had over an hour to wait for the school bus so Peter walked me past the music room and then took me to the library and showed me how to play chess. How the pawns can move forward but never sideways, and the castle in straight lines, and the bishop on the diagonal, and the knight two up and one across, and the king and queen any way they like, only one square at a time for the king, and as many squares as she wants for the queen. I liked that. Peter was good at chess. Not that he said. I saw his name at the top of the cardboard ladder hanging on the wall.

I caught the correct bus home. Peter escorted me to it and saw me safely aboard. Then he walked along on the pavement following my progress until I was seated. And he waved at me through the window. And I waved back.

'How was it?' Aunt Edith asked.

'It was fine. Good even.'

'Did you do all their tests?'

'Yes.'

'And?'

'I don't know. They are going to tell me tomorrow.'

She placed a glass of cold milk and a plate with three biscuits on the kitchen table. 'Come along. Sit down and tell me all about it.'

I hadn't seen her so excited since the day Sister Margaret and Dr Morrison delivered me to her. So I told her everything. All about the tests and Mrs Watts and Peter Hollingsworth. And she smiled from ear to ear and prodded her hair with a finger. Hair that was tied in its usual bun at the back of her head.

'Lovely,' she said. 'Harold will want to hear all about it when he gets in from work.'

The following morning, I walked past the terraced houses in Gladstone Street, along Saddington Road, passing the junior school on the left and the village pond on the right with its weeping willows. I stopped on the High Street, outside the newsagents, where a straggly group of children, dressed exactly as I was, waited for the school bus. I stood on my own, apart from the crowd. Ignored. As if I was invisible. When the bus finally arrived, I let everyone else board before me and took the seat immediately behind the driver where it was empty and quiet. By the time we arrived at school, via the Old Crown, Queen's Head and Coach and Horses, the bus was full and noisy with shouting and screaming and the throwing of various projectiles. We got off in the narrow road next to the playground and I made my way to Mr Hollingsworth's office as I'd been instructed to do the previous day.

'Good morning, good morning,' Mrs Watts said. 'And how are we this morning?'

'I am fine, thank you, Mrs Watts.'

'And didn't we do ourselves proud yesterday. Didn't we. Lovely tests. Just lovely. Mr Hollingsworth was most impressed when he marked them in the afternoon. Most impressed.' And then a strange lady, sitting on one of the chairs outside Mr Hollingsworth's office, her back very straight, said, 'And you, a little . . . well . . . girl from the tropics with no education to speak of. How did you manage it? If Mrs Watts hadn't been supervising I would be wondering who had completed those papers for you.' And then she laughed. So this was just another joke I didn't understand. Who this lady was and what she knew about me and my tests I had no idea. But I don't think Mrs Watts appreciated her contribution either because she didn't smile. Mrs Watts. In fact, she looked quite put out.

The class they assigned me to was 2B, which met for form period in room 6.

'If you make your way down there now they will still be calling the register before assembly. Down the long corridor, on the right.'

I thanked Mrs Watts and set off. When I got to room 6, all the children were seated in little wooden desks that were joined together in twos. The teacher, Mr Butcher, was tall and thin, wearing navy blue trousers and a brown plaid jacket with leather patches on the elbows. Underneath the jacket, a pale blue shirt and green chequered tie that didn't match anything. His black shoes needed a polish.

'Oh, here's our new arrival. Say hello, class.'

'Hello,' they said in unison.

'Hello,' I said quietly, almost under my breath.

'Grab yourself a pew.' He pointed to one of the three vacant seats. It was next to the window on the nearside of the room opposite the door. The girl sitting in the adjacent seat got up and moved to another row so I could have both desks to myself. I sat down and placed my hands together resting on the flat inscribed wood. The letters T and K, either end of an arrow drawn through a heart, which I knew meant 'T loves K'. There were a lot of these. So I reckoned there was a lot of loving going on in the school. Plus, 'Johnny is King' or 'brill' or 'ace', and lots of people who had just written their names, like 'Steve Miller'. Not realising that this was evidence of his guilt. Unless someone else had written it to incriminate him. All I could conclude was that the desk had been there for a long time, and that pupils were more interested in defacing the furniture than paying attention to the history Mr Butcher was teaching them.

'Assembly,' he shouted and everyone rose to their feet and filed out of the room.

The school hall filled quickly, with all the children lining up neatly and the teachers sitting high on the stage. Mr Hollingsworth was seated at the front in the middle while we sang a hymn and a teacher read something from the Bible. And then he watched quietly as different people stepped up to make announcements about returning library books, lost property, tuck-shop hours, after-school clubs, collecting for charity, the vicar's special service at the end of the week and games fixtures. But the strange thing was that the man making the announcement about games was wearing shorts. Not long trousers like the other men, but heavy black cotton shorts, that showed off his very hairy legs. Sister Margaret would never have allowed a thing like that.

So that was how it began. English school. Where, unlike the gentle companionship of Sister Margaret's girls, I had, instead, an endless stream of children who would pull my hair and sting behind my knees with elastic bands or flick the tops of my ears until they were purple and raw. Who would push me to the ground in the crowded chaos between classes, or chase me in the playground shouting their version of monkey noises because they said I had come from the jungle. A boy even threw a banana at me one day. You'd think he would have better things to do with it. Like maybe eat it. Not be wasting it by throwing it at me. Especially since England didn't seem to have any fruit apart from apples and some soft strawberries and raspberries in the summer. Just mushy things like the peas they served with fish and chips. Not anything substantial to sink your teeth into, like a mango or jackfruit. Just apples, and some sour oranges and a few overripe bananas, one of which some idiot decided to throw at me.

Aunt Edith said the children didn't know any better. Poor upbringing at home. I should tell the teachers. I said yes. But I didn't. Peter Hollingsworth said he would watch out for me. But he was in a different class. He was in 2A, which meant he couldn't always be there, no matter how much he wanted to. So he wasn't there the afternoon Evelyn slapped me in the face. A full open-palmed smack against my cheek that landed so hard and loud it made everyone in the French room turn their heads to witness the spectacle.

'Get out!' That is what she said to me as I tried to pack my things together into my satchel. I was standing behind a back-row desk, in front of the chair that she wanted to sit on. The chair she claimed to be her own.

'You are sitting in my chair,' she said.

Without a word of challenge I stood up and prepared to leave. And then I started to say, 'I didn't realise . . .' And that was when she hit me. So I never got to the end of the sentence. 'I didn't realise there were set places.' Because what I had noticed was that children moved around. And I knew for sure I'd seen Evelyn sitting across the room by the window in the previous lesson. Evelyn who could not be missed with her long blonde hair and pack of loud and confident friends. Girls who adored her because she was beautiful and popular with the boys.

'You need to know your place.' She turned to her friends and smirked. 'Where is her place? Where is her place? Who knows where the wog's place is?'

'Back in the jungle,' one of her friends replied.

'On her hands and knees grovelling on the floor,' another one shouted. Just before a third started to honk like a pig. And they all laughed.

'On her knees licking my feet,' Evelyn said to raucous laughter.

'On her knees licking your backside, more like.'

I found a seat towards the front of the class, as far away from Evelyn as possible. But I could still feel her hostility and spite boring into the back of my head. And hear her laughing with her friends. Just the five of them, while twenty or more other children stood around and watched. In silence. So I guess I was the entertainment. The circus monkey. When the teacher arrived, because it was the first period after lunch, I didn't say anything to her about it. It was over. Done. Now it was time for French. Now it was time for the *boulangerie* and the *voiture* and to *tourner à droite vers la gare*.

But that wasn't the worst of it. The shouting and screaming, pulling and shoving and stinging. The worst thing was the spitting. The spitting of slime and sometimes hard balls or runny strings of green phlegm. Spitting in my satchel and on my clothes and in my face. One morning I even returned to my blazer hanging over a chair in the library to find that someone had smeared thick mucus over it. All down the back, from the collar to the hem. What kind of person would make the effort and take the time to do that? Without fearing that they would be caught in the act.

When they started to spit in my hair that was when I asked Aunt Edith to cut it off.

'All of it?'

'As close to my head as possible.' That is what I told her. So I could scrub my scalp and feel cleansed after the daily washing that was now required. Sister Margaret had always combed my hair into little plaits that bobbed and danced as I walked. But Aunt Edith had let my hair grow so now I had it pulled back tight into a bushy sort of ponytail. Tied with a black ribbon. This is what I wanted removed. All of it. All of that curly top.

'But what on earth will you look like?'

'I don't care. Not nobody looking at me anyway,' I said, using the Jamaican voice I hadn't used in months.

'Would you like me or Uncle Harold to go and talk to the headmaster? Sister Margaret thinks it is a good idea as well.'

'No. Then someone will get into trouble. And that will just give them another reason to hate me.' I thought for a moment and then I said, 'You heard from Sister Margaret?'

'Every few weeks we exchange news of you, my dear.'

'Every few weeks?' That was nice, to know that Sister Margaret had not forgotten about me.

What I didn't tell Aunt Edith was about sir and the Thursday afternoon swimming lesson where he would walk to the far side of the pool and tell you to swim the width across to him. And when you got there he would bend down and talk to you. And while you were hanging on the tiled edge he would instruct you about your stroke and breathing, and not bobbing up and down, and conserving your energy. Taking all the time in the world because as long as you were in the water looking up at him squatting on the side like he did, you were staring up into the baggy legs of his black cotton shorts and seeing what he wanted you to see. That he wasn't wearing any underpants.

Well, I'd seen all of that before. Bigger and hairier

than him. And not semi-hard like that neither. Not that I told him that. It wasn't any of my business as long as he kept it to himself, which as far as I was concerned he did. And what he was doing with anybody else wasn't my business either. He could just get his fun from thinking he was surprising me. That was what I thought. But maybe I was wrong. Maybe it was an accident. Maybe he didn't know we could all see what we could see. So that was why I left it alone. Because how could I tell even Aunt Edith a thing like that.

So, anyway, she cut my hair. Aunt Edith. Good and short, and the funny thing was they stopped spitting in it. Most likely it wasn't so much fun any more. Not now that washing out their nastiness would be so much quicker and easier. So, the rest of the term passed a little more quietly than the beginning. Uneventful. And I traipsed from maths to chemistry to history and geography and English and everywhere else with just myself for company. I'd lost my appeal, my fascination. I saw Peter sometimes at break and always at lunch, which they called dinner, and rode the school bus in fear and silence twice a day from Fleckney and back.

Aunt Edith said maybe I could keep a diary. And

each day I could write in it one good thing that had happened. And something I was grateful for. And something I could do to help someone else. And something I could do to make the world a better place. But I couldn't think of anything. Except being grateful. Grateful that she and Uncle Harold had taken me in. I was very grateful for that, even though I would have preferred to stay with Sister Margaret in Jamaica. And be with Gloria and Hyacinth and the rest of the girls. And my baby. But I couldn't. Sister Margaret was in Edinburgh. And even though Gloria and Hyacinth were still in Kingston, my father would have kept coming and taking me away and that was no good. I didn't want to spend another day, not one single day, doing the things I had to do for him. Not another day. Not another hour. Not another minute. Looking up sir's shorts at the swimming pool was plenty enough of that for me.

So I thought maybe I should concentrate on the other things Aunt Edith mentioned. Trying to find one good thing in each day and thinking about how I could help someone else and do something to make the world a better place. And what I thought of was Eric/Ernie and Betsy. And Mr Brown Pants, and Family Need and Greed, and Joan and Stewart and

Mother Glover, and the Sullivans. And especially Him/Her, who must be so very sad in that house all alone, never going out or seeing anybody at all, with no one to talk to or appreciate anything about them or their life. How very sad was that? What could I do to help all of these people who lived side by side in this small circular patch of road, but who seemed to have nothing to do with each other?

England has seasons. Different times of the year that are warm and cold and windy and rainy. When different flowers bloom and leaves turn yellow and then brown and fall to the ground and go brittle and blow unruly around the streets. Or go soggy and mushy and mat together because it rains. It is a country where daylight can last until ten o'clock at night and at another time hardly appear at all, so that it is dark when you leave for school and dark again before you come *home*. That is what I am supposed to call number 24, James Street.

'Home is where the heart is,' Aunt Edith said. But where is my heart? I don't know. If I could have Sister Margaret and Gloria and Hyacinth and all of the girls exactly as we were back in Kingston, and me stay there like that for ever, then that would be home. That is where my heart would be.

'That is not possible,' Peter Hollingsworth said one afternoon, after school, when we were walking back to Fleckney together. Three miles and one hour skirting the edges of planted fields, climbing over wooden stiles and manoeuvring this way and that through metal kissing gates. So Peter said they were called. It wasn't the first time. We would walk to Fleckney and then Peter would catch the bus to Kibworth where he lived with his mother, who was a history teacher in some other school, and his father, our headmaster, and his younger sister, who was still at junior school. A neat and tidy and organised house. That is how I imagined it because of Peter's pressed trousers and smart gabardine blazer, and the knot of his tie always pulled up to his neck, and his clean white shirts, crisp even at the end of the school day when other boys had their tails hanging out and looked worn and crumpled and sweaty from playing football in the playground, with their jackets bundled up and thrown on the ground as goalposts. But not Peter Hollingsworth. He was never anything like that. He was always fresh and ironed like he had just that moment stepped out of the shower and got dressed in the clothes the maid had laid out for him. Not that he ever mentioned a maid. And this wasn't Jamaica, where every *decent* household had one or maybe two living in the outhouse out back with their own bedroom and bathroom and maybe even a little kitchen if they wanted to fix themselves something on their day off. The sort of place I might have lived in if Sister Margaret had put me into schoolgirl service.

So I didn't know anything about the help, but Peter's house was perfect in my mind, with freshly painted windows and doors. And nice curtains hanging in the windows. And a clipped and organised front garden.

'What was the good thing that happened today?'

I thought about it, while matching my steps with his. 'Nobody spat at me.' I let my voice go up at the end like I was asking a question.

'That doesn't count. It has to be something positive.'

'That is positive.'

'You know what I mean.' And then he said, 'All right. Next question. How could you help someone else?'

I thought about the neighbours in James Street that I had been watching all of these months. And then I remembered about Eric/Ernie retiring from the police because of the thing that happened a long time ago.

'Do you know what it was that happened?' I asked.

Peter shook his head. 'It was bad, I know that. Because after he left the police he had to go to the Towers and he was there quite a while.'

We climbed over the final fence and reached the main road.

'What Towers?'

'You don't know? It's the mental hospital. He went mad and they had to put him away.'

'How do you know?'

'My mother told me.'

'What did she have to do with it?'

'She was working at the police at the time. Answering 999 calls. Before she became a teacher. She was the one who took the call when the whole thing kicked off that afternoon.'

'What thing?'

'I don't know. A lot of people ended up dead though.'

'Dead! Did he kill them?'

'No, it wasn't anything like that.'

We headed towards the off-licence. The bell

hanging over the door rang as we went inside. Two packets of potato puffs and a bottle of dandelion and burdock, which we sat on the wall to eat and drink, swigging from the same Whites soft-drinks bottle while we waited for the bus to take Peter home.

Two days later it snowed. Great white flakes that drifted down from the sky looking like the soap powder Aunt Edith used to wash the sweaters she called jumpers. Shetland wool. That is what she said. That needed proper care. But what I didn't know and was to discover, is that snow is wet. Not dry and warm and fluffy like in *White Christmas*, but wet and cold. And when you squish it in your hands it turns to water. And when you walk on it you leave your footprints. Until it melts and goes slushy and dirty and disgusting. Or if it freezes then it's like a sheet of ice that you slip and slide on. All up and down the road that could be the pavement or the strip of grass between the two because you can't see anything but white snow. You can't tell where one thing ends and another begins. And you can't go to school because the bus can't make it along the country road and the teachers are stuck in their own houses and the school caretaker needs helpers to open the building and put on the heating. Nobody cares anyway. All the children want to do is make snowballs and throw them at people in the street.

That was how come Miss Betsy fell over. With her shopping bag. Trying to dodge a snowball. I saw her plain as day from my bedroom window. Saw the cans of soup roll loose into the road and everything else tip out: toilet paper, washing up liquid, cheese, teabags, gravy powder. That is when I rushed out to help her and found the sugar and flour bags damp, and the porridge oats about to burst. And some of the eggs broken. The liquid leaking through the cardboard box told us that. I gathered everything together and put it all back into her shopper.

'Thank you, me duck.' That is what they say here.

'Would you like me to help you inside?'

Miss Betsy didn't answer but she took my hand and led me to the back door, because even though the front door was closer, they always used the back. I'd noticed that.

'Rest everything on the table there if you would.'

I did. Placing down the bag and its soggy contents carefully on the blue Formica kitchen table.

'You sit yourself down and I will make us a nice pot of tea,' and she went to the sink and started to fill the kettle, still wearing her coat and hat, which was more like a knitted tea cosy for keeping the pot warm.

That is how we met. Officially. Not that I drank the tea, but I sat there anyway. And warmed my hands on the chicken-decorated mug while I watched Miss Betsy unpack her shopping and put everything away into her orderly cupboards and tiny fridge that sat under the kitchen counter like a toy. Just like Aunt Edith's. That was also the day I learned to call Miss Betsy, Mrs Watson. And Eric/Ernie, Mr Watson. And that was correct, more respectful, given the difference in our ages and the fact that they were white folk.

When I wanted to go to the toilet I had to walk past the front room and down the corridor, because the house was all on one floor. Not like Aunt Edith's with an upstairs where the bathroom was. But more like a Jamaican house, except with the doors closed. Prim and secretive. The front room door was open though so I saw the fireplace and the mantle above it, and Mr Watson's photograph in its gilded frame. He was wearing his policeman's uniform and pointed hat, looking upright and proud.

It was right after that I started to write my diary, like Aunt Edith said. Something good that happened today. I didn't have to go to school to face those horrible children, and even though it was Thursday, I didn't have to go to the Market Harborough baths for swimming with sir and his baggy black shorts. Good start. Something I am grateful for. Other than Aunt Edith and Uncle Harold. Peter being my friend. Although, strictly speaking, that wasn't a today occurrence because I hadn't seen him. So instead I wrote: Not having been sent to the Towers like Mr Watson. That didn't seem like cheating. After all, I had only just seen his photograph. Something I could do to help someone else. Easy. Helping Mrs Watson to get up out of the street and carrying her shopping indoors for her. Something I could do to make the world a better place. Not so easy. Try to make the street a happier corner of this sad village. Because that is how it always seemed to me. This village. Quiet and still, empty and sad, with a lot of unhappy people. Otherwise why would they talk to me like that?

But if I was going to help other people and the world, then shouldn't I start with me? Because how could I make everybody else happier if I was so very unhappy myself? Wouldn't I have to know how to be happy? So that is how it began, with me changing the way I told Aunt Edith about the things that happened.

The next day when I got back from school and

Aunt Edith asked me how it was I said, 'It was good, Aunt Edith. I learned a lot about electrical conduction today, and how magnesium burns and explodes in water, and how little balls of mercury gravitate towards each other. And I learned about how the square of the hypotenuse is equal to the sum of the squares of the other two sides.' I just reframed the day, refocused it. And even when I talked about the other children, I talked differently about what had happened. Johnny was having a bad day, feeling upset when he shouted at me in the tuck-shop queue. Linda accidently tripped behind me and that was why I fell in the corridor. Elizabeth left a seat for me by the door in the history class because she thought I would be more comfortable there. Graham thought I'd forgotten my satchel so he removed it and put it somewhere safe.

All of which I knew was made up. My own fabrications. Stories I had concocted, which most likely weren't true. But how did I know the truth of anything? Did Johnny say what he did because he hates me? Did Linda deliberately trip me? Did Elizabeth want to show me she was in charge of where I could sit? Did Graham really hide my satchel to be mean? That is what I would have thought in the past. Now all I could say was that things happened. Why? I didn't know. I couldn't guess at people's intentions. But what I could do was make myself feel better by making up happier explanations. Or at least less sad ones. Less hurtful. Less a constant reminder to myself that all of the other children hated me. Even if hate was maybe too strong a word. Did it actually matter whether or not my new stories were true?

Peter took me to Market Harborough library to check the newspapers. Paid the bus fares and even bought us hamburgers and strawberry milkshakes in the Wimpy. It was quite a day out at the old Symington corset factory in Adam and Eve Street. The librarian, Mrs Hallam, was very excited because it meant she could play with her new toy, the microfiche reader, to scan back issues of the *Leicester Mercury*. So she happily scrolled through reel after reel until she found the article – working partly from memory because, according to her, 'Quadruple murders don't happen in Leicester that often'.

'He took it very badly, very badly indeed. I can tell you that for nothing. Not that anybody thought it was his fault. Except him of course. He did. That poor man. Blamed himself from the minute it happened. The minute he got the phone call telling him that everybody in the house was dead. A sorrier sight you couldn't see. Just look at this photograph.'

Getting up close, we peered at the screen. First Peter, and then me. It was Mr Watson on the steps of the police station with a lot of other policemen standing around him looking like they had all seen a ghost.

The story was from 1964 and went like this. At 4.30 p.m. on Friday 24 April, a person calling from a public phone telephoned the police to report a disturbance at their neighbour's house in South Wigston. The call was responded to by PC Watson and PC Lawton. The officers attended the domestic dispute. After a long discussion with the man and woman involved, the officers calmed the frayed tempers and decided that all was under control. When officers were called to the house the following morning, by a neighbour who observed water pouring from under the front door, it was discovered that all inside were dead. The man had suffered a blunt force trauma to the head, while the three children had been drowned and placed in their beds. In their wet pyjamas. Finally, the woman was drowned in the bath with the tap still running. Murder and suicide. That was the verdict.

'That was a terrible thing to have happened,' I said, looking up at Mrs Hallam.

'It certainly was, duck.'

'Is there any more?' Peter asked.

'Only this tiny mention a little while later about PC Watson going to the Towers. Just three short lines. It wasn't news any more after the inquest. It was over and people got interested in something else. A few weeks of excitement that was all it was.' Mrs Hallam turned off the switch on the microfiche reader. The noise and heat suddenly disappeared.

'So, what else can I do for you two this afternoon? Or is that enough information for your school project.' We'd lied. 'Funny thing to want to find out about, if you ask me. Your history teacher must have a warped mind.'

'I've got everything right here,' Peter said, closing his notebook and putting it into his navy canvas duffel bag with the blue Bic he'd used to scribble down the details. Complete with chewed top, which surprised me. Like the bitten fingernails I'd noticed the first time we met and eyed every time we played chess. It didn't seem to go along with the rest of his confident, highly organised, neat and tidy self. Not compatible with the self-assured Peter I knew.

*

'Was it very hard for Mr Watson?'

Miss Betsy nodded as she poured the tea.

'Not that he ever wanted to talk about it.'

'Not even to you?'

'I would be the last person. He feels he let me down.' She took a side glance at me. 'Not just with leaving the police but with the hospital and everything. He never even liked me visiting him there. I still went though. I wanted to see him and the doctors said it was good. To remind him that he still had a life waiting for him.'

I had taken to having afternoon tea with her. Although I was drinking hot chocolate, which was much milkier and sweeter than the cocoa I used to get at Sister Margaret's. Twice, maybe three times a week. She was lonely, Miss Betsy, even though her husband was right there in the house. Or more like in the garden. Planting, weeding, watering, mowing. Bulbs to be lifted and stored. Plants to be removed or repositioned. Seeds to sprout in the greenhouse, seedlings to be picked out and tended. Nursed and nurtured. Feeding and turning the soil, pruning and clearing, cleaning the tools. There was always something to be done. Not just with the lawn and flower beds but with the vegetable plot that yielded so much produce that Miss Betsy kept a wooden crate outside their front gate into which she would put surplus for people to take away. And, after dark, there were seed catalogues to be read.

'He has never been the same.'

'But it wasn't his fault.'

'So they said. But not him. According to him, he should have gone back over there when she called.'

'The neighbour called, didn't he?'

'No, after that. In the evening. When we were sitting in the front room watching the television and the telephone rang and he went out into the hall to answer it and it was her.' I kept my mouth shut and let Miss Betsy carry on. 'And he told her he wasn't on duty. She should ring the station.' She looked over at me. 'But she didn't, you know.' Miss Betsy sipped her tea. 'She just went and did what she did.'

I bit my tongue even though I wanted to ask how the woman had gotten Mr Watson's phone number. But she read my mind.

'He gave her the number that afternoon. When he and Gareth Lawton went over there. Told her she could call him if she wanted to. The poor thing. I think she had really been suffering. Her and the

children, poor little mites. They were all in quite a
state when Eric saw them. But what sense would it
make, calling out social services so late on a Friday
afternoon? Because it had happened before, you
know. Maybe even more than once. And when the
social worker got there, all the mother said was that
everything was all right. Just a little disagreement
between her and the husband. They were fine now.
So what can you do?' Miss Betsy mopped her eye with
the corner of a small, square, cotton handkerchief.
'But Eric won't talk about it. Not to anybody.'

Was she actually crying? I didn't know. Mostly, I
couldn't believe she was telling me all of this. Sharing
her family secrets with an almost complete stranger.
And a child. And a foreigner. An immigrant. Why
would she do that? Maybe it was just a relief to talk
to someone. Somebody who was prepared to listen,
without giving advice or judging her or Mr Watson,
and who wouldn't be going to the Co-op to spread
her woes around the village. She trusted me. Miss
Betsy. That was the point. Even if I didn't understand
why.

'He rang the station, you know. My Eric. After she
telephoned here. And gave them the message. That
she had called him. Passed on that information he

did, to the duty sergeant. I sat in that armchair in the front room and listened to him do it, even turned down the volume on *Coronation Street* so he could hear himself better. But who knows what happened. The next morning, she was gone. And him too and the three children.'

What I realised listening to Miss Betsy is that you never really know someone until you know their story. You never really understand who they are until you understand how they have become the people in their story. Because Mr Eric had gone away into the guilt he felt out of thinking he was responsible. And Miss Betsy had gone away into her sadness out of feeling helpless for not being able to reach out to her husband and make everything better.

But if you can't change the past you can change how you remember it. You can change how you think about it. And if you can do that, you can make up new ways of understanding what happened then and what is happening now. So just like I was making up different stories about what happened at school, a person could do the same thing with their past. They could make the past different, and the present, and the future. Because all of these things are joined together. That is what I decided.

So maybe my mother didn't run away, like my father said, because I was such a bad child. Maybe she had another reason. Maybe she didn't even run away at all. Maybe he left her. And took me with him. For some reason I don't know. Maybe she told him to go and he kidnapped me for the evil he had in mind. And she looked high and low but couldn't find me anywhere because he moved from upcountry to Kingston. So all she could do was miss me, like I miss my baby, because she didn't have anybody to turn to for help. Maybe that is how it was. And I don't have to feel so bad that I was the reason. Being bad from such a young age and carrying on with my badness, which is how I got myself pregnant and Sister Margaret had to take me in. Because even though I said he made me do it, he didn't make me. I did it all myself. I could have said no. I could have run away at any time. And when he came to take me away from Sister Margaret's, I could have refused to go. But I didn't. I went with him, of my own free will.

But maybe that is not how it was. Because what free will does a child have when they are relying on this person to keep a roof over their head and put food on the table? And – as funny as it may seem thinking about my father – protect them? But, more than that, when they are relying on this person to make them feel like they belong somewhere. Like they have family. Because as much as Sister Margaret cared and looked after me, she was not family. He was. And with him was the only place I truly belonged. Until now. Because now I belong with Aunt Edith and Uncle Harold. Officially adopted. Like maybe my baby is adopted and starting a new life with a new family. Not that I know anything about him. But maybe. Maybe one day I will go back to Jamaica and find him or he will come to England and find me. Who knows? Because that is the point. You don't know.

So maybe where you belong has nothing to do with blood. Maybe it is where you are wanted and where people treat you well. Like Aunt Edith showing me nothing but kindness. Maybe it is where you want to give something. Because you care. You appreciate the people around you. Not giving out of a sense of duty or because you think you have to do it to make them love you, because in truth that doesn't really work anyway. But because you want to give. It is a two-way thing and giving makes you feel better. It feels right. You notice the good things that happen each day and you are grateful. You want to help others. You want to add to making the world a better place. Just like Aunt Edith said about me writing in my diary. Even if that world is only a tiny cul-de-sac in a little English country village. It is where we live together and it is somewhere you can begin.

But before I could make a proper plan, Joan and Stewart had left number 22 and the house was boarded up with big pieces of wood nailed across the windows and doors. The council did it, Uncle Harold said, because Mrs Glover shouldn't have been letting that room to them anyway. And now she was dead, the council had taken the house back and didn't want anybody getting in there and either vandalising the place or squatting in it. They hadn't even used proper wood. It was more like sheets of compressed sawdust with all sorts of bits that made it uneven and discoloured. Patchy.

'Why couldn't Joan and Stewart just stay there anyway? They've been living there for years.'

'Because the tenancy was in Mrs Glover's name and you can't just transfer it like that. Joan and Stewart will have to go on the council list in their own name and wait for a house to come up.'

'But their house is empty.'

'Until the council puts someone else to live in there. When they find someone that wants it.' And then he went back to drumming on the kitchen table while reading the *Mirror*, which he wasn't so much reading as staring blankly at the Andy Capp cartoon strip.

I looked at him with the sticks moving up and down in a rhythmic paradiddle.

'You ever think, Uncle Harold, that you might like to join a band?'

'A band?' His hands didn't stop moving. 'And where would I be playing a drum kit around here?'

'I don't mean a big jazz band. Not a full five-piece drum kit and cymbals, hi-hat and all. I mean like maybe a snare drum, like when you marched in the military. Maybe in a brass band. There's loads of them around here.'

'Brass band?' He paused the drumsticks. 'Don't get me wrong, I like the music well enough, but the trouble with brass bands is brass. OK if you play a trumpet or trombone or cornet, there's always two or three of them. But the drums? There's only ever one drummer and those people never give up. I'd be waiting the rest of my life for somebody to die.' And then he started tapping again. But now I could hear the disappointment in his pitter-patter.

I decided not to bother with Mrs Sullivan. Not after what she said to me about playing chess, which was a surprise because she had allowed me to come into their back yard when I first arrived. And play with Stella, even though I didn't quite understand what *playing* we were supposed to be doing. It was more like just hanging around until Mrs Sullivan called Stella in for her *dinner* and shut the back door in my face. I reckoned maybe that was an ordinary, everyday English custom and didn't take offense by it. But the chess thing was completely different.

'You? Playing chess? That is a game for grown men. Intelligent, grown men. Not uneducated, barefoot pickaninnies like you.'

'I am learning at school, Mrs Sullivan, in the chess club.'

'Don't you lie to me, you little scoundrel.' And then she took Stella by the hand and dragged her into the kitchen and closed the door. Maybe it was mean of me to exclude Mrs Sullivan from my new project. But I decided there were plenty other people to think about in the first instance and perhaps I could get to her later.

'What about the children at school?'

'I don't know, Peter. I don't let them upset me

like I used to. I'm even smiling at some of them now. Quite friendly really.' I thought for a while and then I said, 'You are all right. What makes you OK? Why have you been so nice to me?'

He shrugged his shoulders and wobbled his hair. 'I wasn't ever afraid of you.'

'Afraid? Of me? Is that what you're saying? They are afraid of me?'

'Yes, of you being different. Like they only eat certain kinds of food. Potatoes, chops, bacon, fish fingers, tomato sauce, toast, chips. You know. Because anything else would be different, and different equals strange, nasty, disgusting. But, really, it's a kind of defence because they are frightened. And I was never frightened of you.'

'How come?'

'You weren't a surprise to me. You weren't strange. My mum's friend comes from Trinidad. They met when they were 999 operators. She even babysat me a few times when I was younger. So, as far as I was concerned, you were just you, right from the beginning. To be accepted just as you are, without addition or subtraction, multiplication or division.'

*

I started helping Mr Eric in his garden. Just fetching and carrying things. Bring the tray of lobelia or petunia or sweet alyssum. Pass the trowel. Now the fish blood and bone. Now do some watering.

'You see this?' he tugged at the leaves between thumb and forefinger. 'This is a weed. But when you pull it make sure you get the root. Use that hand fork to lift up the soil and gently ease it out, like this.'

Careful, that is how he was. Careful with the mower, up and down the lawn to make visible stripes. Careful with the edge of the beds, so they were sharp and straight. Careful with the paving slabs that were set down with exactly the same twelve inches between each one. Careful with the rows of potatoes and carrots and leeks. Onions, beans, lettuce, radishes. Careful with the tomatoes in the greenhouse. Just like he'd been careful that night to telephone the station. Not that it had done any good.

'Do they get infested sometimes, these plants?'

'Oh, that's a part of gardening. You always have to be paying attention to that.'

'Even no matter how careful you are to make sure everything is just so?'

He rested his weight on the border fork and looked at me. 'No matter how careful.'

'Sometimes things just don't work out?'

He knew what I was talking about. He sat down on a nearby watering stool. The one he used to save his legs on dry summer evenings.

'I did everything except the one thing that was needed of me.'

'Was it needed, Mr Watson? Was it you that was needed?' He looked puzzled. 'You, in the actual flesh. You and nobody else but you? And actually, do we know for sure that anything would have turned out different if somebody, anybody, had gone over there that evening?'

'For certain?'

'Yes, for certain.'

'There isn't anything in this life that is for certain.'

'So, even if somebody had gone over there, even if that somebody had been you, we don't know for certain that come next morning anything would have been different.'

He reached into the pocket of his heavy, brown knitted cardigan and pulled out a ten packet of Player's No 6. Flipped open the lid of the blue-and-white striped box and put a cigarette into his mouth. Then he fetched the matches from his other pocket and lit it. He took a long draw and let the smoke out slowly.

'Maybe not. The way those two were going on, anything could have happened. Sooner or later. Him or her. Either of them.' He took another puff on his cigarette.

'And you couldn't be there. Not every minute of every day you couldn't. Not standing watch over them.'

'It was the children.'

'Was there more to do?'

'Really, when I left, I honestly thought they were all right. They were even laughing and joking, the two of them. That is how all right they were. Standing in the doorway holding the babe on his hip and his other arm around her shoulder. That made such a picture with the other two little ones hanging on to their legs. That was a good ending to a long week for me. And then she rang and I told her I was off duty but if she was worried she should call the station.'

'And you called the station yourself.'

'I did, but why bother giving the woman the number if I had no intention of going over there?'

'Did she ask you to come over?'

He paused and looked over towards me with

startled eyes. 'No, she just said he'd been out and come back drunk and she walked to the phone box to call me because she wanted to get away from him.' Then he looked straight at me and said, 'Nobody ever asked me that before. They asked me what happened and if I'd written everything in my report. But nobody asked me if she'd actually asked me to go over there.' He put the cigarette back into his mouth. After he blew out the smoke, he said, 'I always thought it was my fault, but how could I have known?'

Mr Watson picked up the border fork and pressed it into the garden bed with a little help from his right foot. 'The other thing no one ever asked me was why I had given her this phone number.' He motioned his chin towards the house. 'Not one of those doctors who were busy asking me how I felt and if I was hearing voices or wanted to kill myself. But you know what? If they had, I wouldn't have had an answer for them. I guess I just felt sorry for her. I wasn't thinking beyond that.' And then he turned the soil. 'They said I was depressed and put me on all sorts of tablets. And then they said I was better and sent me home.'

When I looked up, I saw Miss Betsy watching us from the kitchen window. With a smile on her face.

*

I could reach out and touch people. That is what I realised. So, I started to write notes, decorated with carefully drawn and coloured flowers and vines all around the edges. On the pure, white, bond paper Aunt Edith had bought for me. And I put them through the letter boxes early in the morning before I went to school.

To Mister Brown Pants I wrote: *The world belongs to us as much as we belong to it*. To Family Need and Greed I wrote: *If you remove the broken-down car from your front garden we will be able to see your beautiful smiles*. To Him/Her I wrote a question: *Are people meant to live so completely alone?* And I kept doing it. Not every week, just once in a while. Like another time, I wrote to Mr Brown Pants: *The past is gone but the future is still to come*.

And then I watched. Drank hot chocolate with Miss Betsy and helped Mr Eric in his garden. Until finally, one Saturday morning I was gazing out of my bedroom window when I saw Mr Brown Pants walking to the village. But he wasn't Mr Brown Pants any more. He was wearing a pair of denim jeans. Not bright blue, dark. Dark, dark blue, but jeans none-theless. Unmistakable. And as he passed my window he looked up from across the street and smiled. A real, actual honest-to-goodness smile. Not to me, because he couldn't see me through the net curtain. But to the thought of me, because he knew where the notes were coming from.

And after that, marvellous things happened. Family Need and Greed removed the Zephyr car and even tidied their front yard a little, cutting the waist-high grass and trimming the pink rambling rose that grew on the wire fence at the side of their house. Then one afternoon I came back from school to discover that I had a note. Posted to me in an envelope with a stamp, which Aunt Edith had opened because it didn't have a name on it, just our address. It was a white index card, six by four inches, and it read: *If they choose to.* So, the next morning, I went straight away to Him/Her at number 20 and left my reply: *But what would make someone choose to do that?*

But one of the very best things to happen was Peter telling me that Kibworth brass band was looking for a drummer.

'Really? Kibworth? Three miles away? A drummer?'

'Kibworth. Practically on Uncle Harold's doorstep. Seems the man is moving to Newcastle or some such place. Mrs Burgess told me.'

'Who is Mrs Burgess?'

Peter looked embarrassed. Almost guilty. 'She's just a lady who helps at my house. You know with the cleaning and washing, ironing, things like that.'

So I was right, he does have a maid. 'Does she sleep at your house? Out back?'

'No,' he said, almost like he was shocked or offended. 'She just comes three times a week.'

'You have something to say?' She was edging her way closer to the counter. In the Co-op., where I was waiting to pick up a few items for Miss Betsy. And actually I did have something to say because I thought I was next in the queue.

Mrs Gaskell stood there like she didn't know who to serve next. Except she did know it was me. Surely she did. I had been waiting for ages.

'Say it then! Spit it out.' The woman tugged the arm of her little girl, pulling her closer while continuing to creep towards the counter. The child looked about five years old. And terrified. I opened my mouth but nothing came out.

'Some people need to learn some manners,' she said, as if to the girl, but loud enough for the whole store to hear. 'Don't they? Need to learn some manners. That is what they need to do. Learn some manners.'

She stared at me. So intently it was as if her eyes were burning into my very being. I exchanged glances with the girl who looked like she was expecting me to lash out at her grandmother or whoever this woman was to her.

'You have something to say to her? You want to ask the child something? Go on then, she speaks English.'

I kept my mouth shut but couldn't stop my anxiety and humiliation from shuffling my feet on the spot.

'Some people need to learn some manners.'

And then I heard a man's voice coming from somewhere deep in the store. 'That is enough.' When he stepped out from behind the aisle of cans I saw who it was. It was the eldest son of Family Need and Greed. He strolled over to us and said it again. 'That is enough. You have no right to talk to her like that. She is my neighbour. And she was waiting here long before you. Apologise to her or get out.'

The woman looked like she wanted to hit him. But she didn't. She just turned and walked out, dragging the child behind her.

Big Son fingered and fiddled with various items

while Mrs Gaskell served me and then he said, 'Come on, I'll walk you home.'

'Home?'

'To James Street. Number 24. That is where you live, isn't it? With your mum and dad.'

I just looked up at him and said, 'Yes.'

And as we walked up Gladstone Street, him with his hands in his pockets like Uncle Harold says you shouldn't, he turned to me and said, 'So what's your name anyway?'

Times and Seasons

Carolyn Sanderson

CAROLYN SANDERSON has worked in a number of fields, including teaching, training, counselling, academia and the Church of England. She has written articles, reviews and a number of hymns, and lives in Milton Keynes.

Author's Note

I wasn't born in Milton Keynes – indeed, the new town didn't exist when I was born – but I have lived there for longer than I've lived anywhere else and so for me now it is home.

People who have never been to visit often have a woefully mistaken view of the place we call the New City: a shiny, soulless planner's dream, maybe, or a repository for people who can't afford to live in London. But it is so much more than that, with a history and character and life of its own. Its famous grid square system encompasses areas still under construction as well as places that have been there for thousands of years.

Mattie and Paul's story in *Times and Seasons* is entirely fictional, although the places and some of the events described are real, including the reburial of the Saxon bones. While the characters in the dream sequences are not documented individuals, I have tried to be faithful to the times they lived in, giving them names and experiences that reflect the history of the area around Milton Keynes Village. All Saints Church is still there, too, alive and well and over seven hundred years old.

Once you start looking, there are many other ancient settlements to be uncovered, but Milton Keynes Village is the one I know best. I have chosen to weave my story around this particular place, which I have come to love and where I am constantly made aware that we are all part of something much, much bigger than ourselves.

Carolyn Sanderson, January 2018

THERE ARE MEN in the village again, strangers. They come on horseback, with measuring sticks, and they speak in the tongue of the invaders. I watch from behind my mother's skirts as they move to and fro, calling to each other, making a tally of our fields and pathways. Then they are gone and we are left alone again with our Saxon tongue and the hard labour of a harvest to get in before the rains.

My father spits in the dirt. 'They'll be back,' he says, his voice bitter, 'back to collect their taxes, now they've seen what we've got.'

On Our Lady's feast day we go to church and my mother cuffs me for crying over a grazed knee when I should be silent and respectful. Father Osric utters magical words in another foreign tongue: HOC EST CORPUS MEUM. As the bell rings we bow our heads and I know that God is in our midst, though I cannot see

*him. My brother Aegfrith pushes me in play as we leave. I
try to stop my fall with my hands, scraping them against
the rough wood of the church wall. A splinter lodges under
my skin, which makes me cry again.*

*Holy day or no holy day, there is work to be done if we
want to eat this winter, and from my hiding place behind
the barn, I watch as men and women head to the fields to
cut down great stalks of wheat and barley while the sun
casts its golden light above.*

*I know that I should help my mother but the house
is smoky from the fire and it makes my eyes water. The
workers will be hungry when they come back. Aegfrith has
gone with them. He is twelve now, almost a man grown.
It surprises me to find I miss him.*

*The sunshine is warm and I doze, half hearing the men
calling to each other across the field, and in the distance
the faint lowing of the cattle. Sometimes I think they are
white cows with black patches, but at others they seem to
me black cows daubed with white. I wonder if they know
they will soon be brought into our houses to keep us warm
with their hot breath and steaming bodies.*

*I open my eyes. Above my head the sky is deepest blue,
and I feel that I can see into heaven itself. Does God look
back down at me? What would Father Osric say if I told
him this? What can a girl know about such things? Sleep*

drifts heavily around my head and, as my eyes close, I hear ever more faintly the sounds of the harvest, the cows, the cry of the gulls, winging and wheeling above the midden . . .

Milton Keynes Village, 2012

AND NOW I am awake, but barely, in that warm space where the dreams I have left feel real. It is as though the girl in the dream is both me and not me. But this is not the eleventh century, I tell myself, and the cry of the gulls that echoes in my ears is real. For a moment I think it is a seagull, but I am a long way in time and space from my childhood home in Liverpool. Not a seagull, then: a gull. Finally, I am fully awake, and I remember why today is special.

Cautiously, on one elbow, I survey my new bedroom, still untidy from last night's rushed unpacking. I'm nervous, of course: a new job is always nerve-wracking, and when it's more than a job, when it's a vocation . . . The sense of responsibility weighs heavy, but there are other reasons beyond that, beyond the upheaval of the move; this new phase in my life comes freighted with old memories.

I force myself from the warmth of my bed. The central heating has switched itself on, making the room stuffy. I will have to adjust it or I'll never manage to get up for the early services. Another new thing to learn.

Along the passage is my study, the place that will become my sanctuary. It's all still here, just as I left it. My pictures hang on the walls and my books stand in rows on the shelves. This is no dream.

I'm not hungry but know I should have some breakfast. It's important to be at my best for the meetings that lie ahead today. Unseen hands have furnished my cupboards with the bare essentials: bread and milk, eggs, tea and coffee, as well as the inevitable lemon drizzle cake. It seems to be a speciality in every parish I've served in. I crack two eggs into a pan, scrambling them quickly, and then carry my breakfast out onto the little terrace. I bless my predecessor silently for leaving behind a table and two chairs. Such a glorious way to start the day: in the sunshine with the greens and blues of nature so vivid and intense. I hear my neighbour's car start up and am thankful that he can't see me as I sit here in my pyjamas, hidden behind the willow screening and the pot plants that were parting gifts from friends up North.

I lift a forkful of egg to my mouth and am instantly transported back to the very first time I came to this place. I am eighteen again, and it is the first full week I've ever spent away from my parents. I can no longer resist the crowding memories.

Broughton Village, 1987

AUNTIE GRACE MADE the best scrambled eggs in the world: soft, creamy and a rich, deep yellow. I tumbled out of bed on the first morning of my stay and ate a plateful hungrily. I was wondering whether I could ask for more when Paul came in, half-dressed, his hair tousled. I blushed and looked away. This was a new thing between us. When we were little and his parents came to visit, he was a nuisance – I couldn't see the point of him or of boys in general, with their blundering and shouting and the fighting games that always ended in tears. Paul never wanted to play at nursing sick dolls or spying fairies in the garden. But now we were older, we were allies against an adult world that didn't understand us – our parents least of all. And Paul was a great support in my campaign to be allowed more freedom. It had taken quite some effort.

*

I had always thought of Liverpool as a place it was impossible to escape from. My father refused to go on holiday and wouldn't even make the journey down to Milton Keynes, so Auntie Grace, Uncle Albin and Paul always had to come to us. When they visited at Christmas the year before Paul and I sat our A levels, we were fretting over textbooks and filling in UCCA forms. I had my fingers crossed for good enough results to get into Southampton or Exeter or Newcastle (all carefully chosen for their distance from Liverpool). Paul used the opportunity to start petitioning Mum and Dad to let me go and stay with them in the summer. He said it would be good preparation for university life and that Auntie Grace and Uncle Albin could be trusted to look after me like their own. Amazingly, my parents said yes!

My friends back home laughed when I told them that I was going to spend my week's holiday – my reward for working so hard at my A Levels – in Milton Keynes.

You're joking!

No way!

They don't have real animals, just concrete ones!

A concrete jungle!

Hahaha!

But I wasn't going for the scenery, and I didn't envy Bella or Lizzie or Cathy when they told me about their package holidays abroad. Sunshine, adventure, no adults: I knew that my parents would never have let me do that. After they lost Claire, the world became a threatening place: if only they hadn't allowed her to play out that day; if they'd kept her inside the house; if they'd been watching... I was their only child now, the only one there would ever be, and that was what made them cocoon me in cotton wool.

Mum and Dad trusted me to Auntie Grace because she understood their fears in a way no one else could. She was Mum's best friend at school, and even though she had left Liverpool to settle in the place where her own parents had been born, she and Mum remained very close. She came at once when she heard about Claire. She was there at the hospital and then later at the undertaker's. She had sat with my parents, listening patiently through the tears, through the silences. On the day my mother found out she was expecting me, it was Auntie Grace who had persuaded her that, yes, she could do it; she could be a good mother to another child. Paul was born a few months before me and I felt he must have been listening while Auntie Grace was holding my mother's hand and talking gently about new life and the future. Maybe that's why we had felt some sort of connection from the beginning, as if we truly were cousins, as if our mothers really were sisters.

I was excited but a bit surprised when Paul, who had only passed his driving test the year before, arrived to collect me. Why my Dad thought I was safer being driven by an eighteen-year-old male on a motorway than sitting on a train, I don't know. Even though I was brought up in a big city, my experience of it was limited to the bus journey to school and back and an occasional trip to the shops with Mum. I was never allowed to take the train by myself. While my friends went clubbing at weekends, I stayed at home. I once tried going to a pub with Cathy while Dad thought we were revising. It was loud and crowded and really exciting; some lads at the next table were definitely eyeing us up. But when I got home my clothes smelled of cigarette smoke so I had to admit where I'd been and that was the end of any outings for me.

Being driven by Paul felt like an adventure – like I'd finally slipped the net – but when we arrived and

I saw where they lived, I was disappointed. I had imagined that Broughton was a district in the great metropolis of Milton Keynes, but it turned out to be a tiny village in the middle of nowhere – a few old houses and no street lighting. So much for the new town I'd been promised!

After breakfast on my first morning, Paul asked me what I'd like to do. I wasn't used to being given choices and told him I was up for anything. We set off on foot, down a winding country lane and across a stream until we came to a large thatched building. I turned to Paul.

'Where have you brought me? What happened to the bright lights of MK?'

'This is Milton Keynes. *The* Milton Keynes.'

There was a half-grin on his face. He always struggled to keep a straight face when he was playing some sort of joke on me, but I couldn't quite work out what he was getting at here.

'Where do you think MK got its name from?'

'Well, from one of England's greatest poets, obviously.' I was proud of this piece of knowledge. We'd studied *Paradise Lost* for A Level. 'And, er...' I was on less sure ground when it came to Keynes. 'The economist guy?'

'Aha! No – that's what everyone thinks, but you're wrong on both counts.' He waited for my reaction. I waited for him to stop waiting. 'Don't you want to know?'

I didn't want to give him the satisfaction, so I carried on, striding along the lane as it narrowed and became quite overgrown in places. I glimpsed other buildings in the distance, some of them thatched, others dark with ivy clinging to the crumbling red bricks. I stumbled as my foot got caught on a bramble, the thorns biting into my skin.

'All right,' I said, turning to Paul. 'I give in. Are you going to tell me?'

He didn't answer right away, savouring the moment, I suppose. Instead he carried on walking until we reached an old stone church. It looked a bit like a mother hen with her chicks, crouching there amongst the gravestones. The heavy wrought-iron gate creaked on its hinges and then clanged shut behind us as we passed from the lane into the church-yard. I got a stone in my shoe walking along the loose gravel path and had to hop while I took it off and shook out the offending fragment. Paul held my arm to stop me falling over. I realised that I liked the feel of his firm grip, even if I was still a bit cross with him.

'Well?'

'This village has been here since before William the Conqueror. It's listed in the Domesday Book. There were three small settlements, or "tons": this was the middle one, so it was Middle-ton, Middeltone, and that got shortened to Milton.'

'And then they added the Keynes bit?'

'Yes, later. One of the big families was the de Cahaignes.' He spelt it out for me. 'There were other spellings, of course. English spelling wasn't standardised in those days.'

I knew that, and anyway, I'd already figured out that the name wasn't English with that 'de' in front of it. I said so.

'Quite right. It was a Norman-French name.'

I tried to ignore the patronising note in his voice. It was one of the things that had annoyed me when we were younger and bickered as though we were brother and sister.

'They must have come over with William or one of his successors.'

'What?' I had drifted off into my own thoughts and

it took me a moment or two to realise that Paul was still delivering his lecture.

'The de Cahaignes. The King rewarded the barons who supported him by giving them land, even if it already belonged to someone else.'

'What are you – my history teacher?'

'If I was I'd make sure you knew something about history.'

I'd had enough of this, so I crunched over the gravel until I reached the huge iron-hinged door to the church. There was a notice with the name of the Church: All Saints, and another saying where we could get a key to go inside.

'Do you want to go in?' Paul asked from behind me.

I did and I didn't. It was July and the sun was already high and hot – one of those days where the sky is blue and cloudless and the very air shimmers with heat. I felt as though I could see into heaven itself. Did I really want to go into a dim stone building on such a glorious morning? Yet I felt drawn to the place, too. It was ancient, more ancient than the houses and the country lane and the bridge we'd crossed, and I thought about the centuries it had stood there, a silent witness to the passage of time, to people so unlike us, and yet so like us too.

We walked all the way round the outside. There was a sort of ditch, about a metre wide, hollowed out between the walls and the level of the graveyard. Paul thought it was something to do with stopping the damp getting in, but I think he made that up and didn't really know the answer. He was a bit like that: he knew a lot of things, and being confident came naturally, so you couldn't always tell if he really knew or was just guessing. He told me it was over seven hundred years old, which I found out later was true.

It was built of great blocks of stone, some of them crumbling a bit. After so long, that was no surprise. I wondered what our Victorian terrace back in Liverpool would look like after a few hundred years.

The church didn't have a spire; those were a later development. It had a tower instead, a square one, positioned halfway down one side. I found myself stroking the stones, absorbing their antiquity and trying to imagine what the church might have been like when it was new. I wondered about the people, and in my mind I vaguely saw the ladies in their flowing dresses and the men in — what would they have worn? Hose? Chain mail? I was starting to wish that I had chosen history as one of my A Levels.

'Can we go and get the key now?' I asked Paul.

'It's OK. I'll go and get it; you stay here.'

He left me in a heavily shaded part of the church-yard, beneath some dense, dark yew trees that rose dramatically from the ground and met far above my head. I reached for the tufts of soft leaves that grew all the way up and shivered. They were cold to the touch. Church wasn't something that happened in my family. Auntie Grace said it was after Claire died that my parents stopped going. They were angry with God, and that was why there was no religious funeral, no ashes in a churchyard.

This sense of otherness was new to me. I found the idea of belief and ritual intriguing, but in the abstract, hence choosing Religious Studies as an A Level. My little act of rebellion.

In the oldest part of the churchyard, the grave-stones were flaking with age and I couldn't read them. I found myself wondering about the people whose names had been carved there so many years before. When people say, 'it isn't carved in stone,' they mean to suggest impermanence, but here were the precious names of loved ones carved on stone, and yet no more

permanent than anything else. I felt sad for these unknown people, and something else besides, as though
I had somehow moved out of time, or beyond it.

Then the moment was gone, interrupted by Paul
sauntering along the path with a large but disappointingly modern-looking key. He had to rattle
it in the lock a few times before the heavy wooden
door swung inwards and the cool, dark interior once
more swept me backwards in time. It struck me that
the musty air could have been trapped for centuries. I
coughed a little as I inhaled the dust. There was such
stillness there. In front of us the old Victorian font
stood proud on its stone plinth. The windows were
mostly clear diamonds of glass, but at one end the
sunlight picked out rows of coloured pictures: a comic
book for people unable to read words. I resisted the
impulse to ask Paul to explain them to me.

He steered me into a little side chapel, which
seemed to be part storeroom and part meeting room,
although I wouldn't have wanted to sit on any of
those old canvas chairs smelling of damp.

'This used to be the schoolroom,' he said. 'Back
in Victorian times,' he added, before I could ask
if it was where he had gone to school. He showed
me some flat pieces of lead, with names and dates

on them. 'Seventeenth-century graffiti.' I laughed, and he explained that they must have been marked by workmen mending the roof centuries ago. I tried to imagine them, high above the fields and village rooftops as they worked, scratching their names in an idle moment. Running my fingers over the writing, I shivered a little, but I was glad they had found a way to be remembered.

We went back to the house for the car and were soon on a dual carriageway, whizzing past trees and green spaces, like little parks running alongside. The roads intersected neatly at right angles, converging into roundabouts that all looked the same to me. Paul missed his turning once and we circled around several times, so I think they must have looked similar to him too.

'But where is it?'

'What?'

'Milton Keynes!'

'Here! You're in it. Behind the trees.' He grinned. 'Honestly – I'm not pulling your leg. It's just that they designed it this way, so each grid square is self-contained.' He seemed to hesitate for a moment. 'OK, look, I'll show you.' He took a turning down a slip road, and suddenly we were in a broad, tree-lined avenue, with smaller roads branching off it at right angles. The houses looked like something out of a magazine.

'Wow – this is different!'

I thought of the rows and rows of terraced houses back home, the treeless streets, the scrawny parks with nothing in them but stunted bushes and vandalised benches. I couldn't remember passing a single green plant as my bus crawled to school every day in nose-to-tail traffic. Paul had never once been forced to stop since we set off.

About halfway down the avenue, Paul turned into a kind of square, with a Tesco's and a chippie, a chemist, off-licence and what looked like a village hall. He pulled into a parking space, but when I asked if his mum wanted us to get some shopping, he laughed.

'Come on! Don't spoil my official tour-guide act. You wanted to see where Milton Keynes is – well here we are!'

'This can't be it. It's too small.'

He laughed again. 'This is a local centre. All the grid squares have one.'

Local centre? Grid squares? I wasn't really getting

it, but I got out of the car and looked around a bit to humour him.

'Are you ready to go on now?' he asked, sensing I was bored.

'More than ready,' I replied, already walking back to the car.

Paul swung himself into the driver's seat and threw the car into reverse, slamming his foot down on the accelerator harder than was necessary. 'You want excitement? I'll give you excitement!' The wheels threw up a shower of small stones as he hurled the car out of the parking space.

Scared and excited at the same time, but not wanting him to think I was impressed, I turned to him with a withering glance, 'Well, that won't do your mum's tyres any good, will it?'

Back out on the road we joined another of the big dual carriageways, winding our way up a series of bends towards what I took, at first, to be a shining hilltop city, like in a fairy tale. It wasn't any such thing, of course, and when we finally reached it, Paul eased the car in alongside hundreds of others and I could see that it was an unbroken line of shops roofed under chrome and glass. This was more like it! He turned to me with a wide grin, his good humour fully restored now he could see I was impressed.

'Largest shopping centre in Europe!' he announced, as though it was all his own work. I leapt out of the car.

After we'd looked in a few of the shops, we ate lunch in the atrium, perched next to the shiny tropical plants and trees that pushed up into the clear glass of the roof space. Birds twittered and cheeped above us, amongst what I took to be palm trees, and I could swear that there were little bunches of green bananas on them.

The juices oozed out of the quarter-pounder Paul had bought me. By the time I had half eaten it, my hands and chin were greasy and I didn't care. This was not the sort of food I was allowed back home, but here I was a different person, more daring, more alive. Reaching out for my chips – fries – I knocked the carton with my elbow and they went tumbling into the dark green foliage behind us. I wasn't sure what to do. Paul laughed and said by the look of some of those plants they would probably eat them for us, and we laughed, and then he shared his fries with me. When we came to the last one we both made a grab for it and our fingers touched. Paul took it and broke it in two. One half he placed carefully in his own mouth, and the other he pushed, slowly and deliberately, between my lips. I stared at him and forgot to chew. He really did have the most wonderful eyes, and they were laughing at me again.

I'd never really had a boyfriend. Steve didn't count because he had only walked me home from the youth club dance once and he hadn't even tried to kiss me goodnight. And with Jonny it was all on my side; he had no idea that I fancied him.

Just before Paul leaned forward and kissed me on the mouth, I had a quick debate with myself. I wasn't sure if this was all right, but I decided to worry about that afterwards. Afterwards, I sort of forgot to worry about it.

He held my hand on the way to The Point. I can't remember which film we chose. A day earlier and I'd have been overawed by the series of cinemas within a cinema, in a building that looked like a neon tomb for a trendy pharaoh. The smell of roasting popcorn thickened the air and there were so many people rushing about and shouting, but I was oblivious to it all. Paul held my hand as we presented our tickets at the little lectern-desk and went into the darkness where the adverts boomed out. We sat at the back and watched very little of the film.

That night the dreams began.

The weave of my tunic is rough against my skin. I am with my people in the village that is to become Milton Keynes. Beyond the cluster of crudely finished huts is a larger building, more carefully finished than the others, its planks smoothed and fitted together without gaps. There is fear in the air. We carry hoes and pitchforks, but we are not working in the fields. These are weapons, and it is not only the men who carry them. We bow our heads as horsemen thunder into the village. They speak to us harshly, issuing orders and demands that we can't understand. One of them, clearly more important than the rest, rides a tall black horse that stares down at us as haughtily as its rider. We are all afraid, and at length we bow our heads and drop our implements.

When I awoke I found the roughness of my tunic still chafed my skin and the words of the important man on the horse rang in my ears, although I could no more understand them then than in the dream. He seemed powerful, as he sat there astride, his cloak whipping around his shoulders in the breeze. Birds sang in that

long-ago time and place, just as they do n
everything else was utterly different. My pe
been made subservient. I felt sad that they h
so cowed by their overlords, although a littl
too, that they had enough spirit to attempt re
In the dream, I looked up and saw that atop tl
wooden building there was a cross. I wond
could have been a church, although it was notl
the one Paul had taken me to.

Groggily, I came to and took in Auntie
busy guest room with the light filtering
flower-patterned curtains and scattering
my bed. I heard Uncle Albin's alarm cl
out. I knew I was firmly back in the twenty—f
tury.

Albin always got up early, even at the
when he didn't have to. After a while I he
moving about downstairs and then I must hav
back to sleep again because the next thing I h
raised voices.

'You think I make all this sacrifices all th
so you go waste yourself? You got chances I
and you want to throw it all away . . .' Albin
became more pronounced and harder to unde
his voice rose, but there was no mistaking his

where the adverts boomed out. We sat at the back and watched very little of the film.

That night the dreams began.

The weave of my tunic is rough against my skin. I am with my people in the village that is to become Milton Keynes. Beyond the cluster of crudely finished huts is a larger building, more carefully finished than the others, its planks smoothed and fitted together without gaps. There is fear in the air. We carry hoes and pitchforks, but we are not working in the fields. These are weapons, and it is not only the men who carry them. We bow our heads as horsemen thunder into the village. They speak to us harshly, issuing orders and demands that we can't understand. One of them, clearly more important than the rest, rides a tall black horse that stares down at us as haughtily as its rider. We are all afraid, and at length we bow our heads and drop our implements.

When I awoke I found the roughness of my tunic still chafed my skin and the words of the important man on the horse rang in my ears, although I could no more understand them then than in the dream. He seemed powerful, as he sat there astride, his cloak whipping around his shoulders in the breeze. Birds sang in that long-ago time and place, just as they do now, but everything else was utterly different. My people had been made subservient. I felt sad that they had been so cowed by their overlords, although a little proud, too, that they had enough spirit to attempt resistance. In the dream, I looked up and saw that atop the larger wooden building there was a cross. I wondered if it could have been a church, although it was nothing like the one Paul had taken me to.

Groggily, I came to and took in Auntie Grace's busy guest room with the light filtering through flower-patterned curtains and scattering across my bed. I heard Uncle Albin's alarm clock ring out. I knew I was firmly back in the twenty-first century.

Albin always got up early, even at the weekend when he didn't have to. After a while I heard him moving about downstairs and then I must have drifted back to sleep again because the next thing I heard was raised voices.

'You think I make all this sacrifices all these years so you go waste yourself? You got chances I no have, and you want to throw it all away . . .' Albin's accent became more pronounced and harder to understand as his voice rose, but there was no mistaking his passion.

'Dad, I'm trying to explain...' Paul's voice too was rising. It contained no hint of his usual good humour.

'Right. You go explain to your mother. You tell her she wasting her time doing two jobs, working her fingers bony so you go to that school...'

There was a crash. Something had fallen off the table – or been thrown. Expletives in Uncle Albin's native Polish filled the air, then there were more footsteps and the front door slammed. The silence that followed was nerve-wracking and then I heard the sound of a brush sweeping the kitchen tiles.

I took my time getting up and waited until I heard Paul come back from wherever he had been before daring to go downstairs. Breakfast was eaten in strained silence. I could see that Auntie Grace had been crying, but it didn't seem a good idea to comment on it, especially as there was nothing I could say to make it better. Paul sat, avoiding her gaze. He turned to look at me.

'You coming?'

I slipped from my chair and fetched a cardi. The day had turned a bit cooler.

Paul cleared his throat. 'Is it still all right if I borrow your car to take Mattie out, Mum?' Auntie

Grace nodded, squeezing her hankie in her left hand and picking up her cup with her right. The tea looked as though it had been there a long time, the milk having separated into fatty globules on the surface.

We drove in silence, leaving the system of grid squares behind as we approached a small town. It looked like a pleasant enough place, although disappointingly ordinary with a main street lined with little shops and pubs.

Paul pulled sharply into a car park, spraying a few loose bits of gravel before coming to rest under a sign that said, 'Free Parking: Long Stay'. We sat there awkwardly for a while until I summoned the courage to ask – tentatively – what was wrong.

'Oh, I've let everyone down. I've done nothing but take and I'm basically just a selfish bastard.' He was glaring at the steering wheel as though it had wronged him.

'I know your dad's angry with you. I could hear him shouting; but what have you actually done?'

'Told them the truth. Told them I don't want to go to uni, don't want to carry on with this education conveyor belt.' He looked out of the window, bleakly.

'And they've told me how much of a disappointment I am.'

'Paul.' I touched his arm, still timid with him. 'You're head boy. You're predicted As. They're so proud of you.'

'Proud of me so long as I follow the path they've got mapped out for me.'

I took a deep breath. It's so easy to see things when it's not your own life that's crashing about you in ruins.

'I can see where your dad's coming from. He arrived in this country with nothing, a refugee—'

Paul grimaced and I wondered if I should have said 'migrant' instead. Uncle Albin used to tell stories about his homeland and how it was taken by the Russians at the end of the Second World War, how the people had been subjected to a regime that his parents bitterly opposed. I ploughed on.

'He had to work incredibly hard. He married your mum. They managed to get a mortgage. They scrimped and sent you to a good school. They wanted you to have a better life than theirs ... They're disappointed *for* you, not by you.'

'Hmm.'

There was silence. I risked another tack.

'I thought you were really keen to go to uni. You're mad about history. You've been talking about studying it for years.'

'I've *been* studying it for years. I've done everything that's expected of me. I've jumped through the hoops. And now I've had enough.' There was a pause. 'Anyway, who knows? I might not get the grades!' He was flippant, as if he didn't care – but then offered me that lopsided smile, the one that gets me every time. 'This place isn't going to explore itself. Let's go, girl.' He swung out of his seat with an approximation of his usual energy, coming round to my side to open the door before I could fully shake myself into a mood to match his.

We set off down the street with its perfectly nice but unexciting shops: a butcher's and a cake shop and a little gift shop, a couple of charity shops.

'It'll blow over,' Paul said, slipping a comforting arm around my shoulders. Then he stopped. 'Look there.' He pointed across the street to an old building coated in a pinkish plaster with a plaque high up on the wall. 'There – see? Richard III was here before us!'

I read the plaque. Richard, Duke of York, had rested here on his way to London with the princes, his brother's children. I may not have known much history, but I knew that these were the Princes in the Tower.

Paul broke into my thoughts. 'And who knows what happened to them? Political pawns. They had no choices, just because of who their father was.' The thought hung in the air.

We strolled on. Paul pointed out the high archways at intervals along the street.

'This was a coaching town. These were all inns – see? That's where the horses and carriages went through to the inn yards. It was on the road to London, so a good stopping-off place.'

'What's it called? Are we still in Milton Keynes?'

He laughed. 'That's a moot point. The people of Stony Stratford like to think they're quite separate from the hoi polloi in the new town.' He stopped again and pointed. We were outside a couple of pubs, both showing evidence of the high-arched entrances. 'Have you ever heard the expression "a cock and bull story"? Well, this is where it comes from.'

I looked to where he was pointing, and saw that one of the pubs was called The Cock and the other, a very short distance away, was The Bull.

'Oh, I see. If you visited both, you might well end up talking nonsense.'

'You got it!'

We wandered on, past more quaint old buildings. Paul took me through to the Market Square, where Charles Wesley had preached, underneath an ancient elm tree. I tried to appear suitably impressed. I hadn't known trees could live that long.

The sun was shining now and Paul was starting to relax again. We passed a coffee shop, wedged between the post office and a craft shop and, without needing to consult one another, went in. It felt good to be sitting there with him, miles from home, knowing, or at least hoping desperately, that I would soon be escaping my family to go to university. I couldn't really understand why Paul didn't want the same, but then I had a sudden insight: was Paul also seeking freedom? Not freedom to *do*, as I was, but freedom to *be*? Freedom to find out who he was, to escape from the expectations his parents had of him?

Idly, I watched as people passed the window: family groups, people hurrying in their lunch hour, someone on the way to the post office with a huge parcel. A small child was throwing a massive tantrum. I felt sorry for her harassed-looking mother. A dog came sniffing up to the window before being called away by a shrill whistle from its owner. The coffee had re-energised me and I felt benevolent to all the people out there, living their own lives. My thoughts strayed back to my strange dream and I found myself wondering about the lives of the people who had lived around here so long before us.

'Paul, do you think we could go back to the village this afternoon? There's something I want to look at again.'

Paul's mood had lifted enough for him to tease me. 'Oh yes? Getting hooked on history after all, are you?'

I rolled my eyes. 'Well, you're such a great teacher.' I should have left it there. The last thing I wanted to do was to spoil the mood, but I couldn't resist asking if he'd thought about deferring for a year while he considered his future. He growled a bit until we got back to the car, but promised to think about it. Then we went back to ancient Mideltone.

I tried to find the place I'd seen in the dream, but it all looked so different – and anyway, I had to remind myself, it was only a dream.

'They're going to make a cricket pavilion over there,' Paul said, waving his arm vaguely as we walked through the village. I tried to imagine the scene, although I'd only experienced that sort of thing on TV: a summer afternoon, the players in white, a scattering of spectators in deckchairs, sipping cold drinks and applauding languidly.

I suddenly had that feeling again, the one I'd had in the churchyard. I paused and looked around. Paul was staring at me with consternation.

'Are you OK?'

'What are we standing on, here?'

'Grass? Old common land, possibly. I think this is where they're going to make the car park for the new pavilion.'

A new pavilion didn't remotely explain the strange feeling, but I let it pass. I couldn't have put it into words if I'd tried.

At dinner no one spoke while we ate the rich beef stew Auntie Grace had made, and the awkward silence continued even after she brought her renowned apple pie to the table. I must have looked particularly miserable, as Paul took it upon himself to pull a funny face at me. I choked and had to be patted on the back by Uncle Albin. That broke the ice a bit, enough at least for Auntie Grace to start a conversation.

'Have you seen the concrete cows yet?'

I shook my head. 'I've heard of them.'

'No?' Uncle Albin appeared shocked and turned – for the first time during the meal – to his son. 'You must take her see the concrete cows, tomorrow, Paul.'

I worried that Paul would refuse, just to be difficult, but to my relief he accepted his dad's peace offering, and deliberately asked his advice about what else we should see.

'You should go see Willen Lake,' he advised, 'and the Grand Union Canal, and Linford Wood, and...'

'That will take more than a morning!' Auntie Grace said, and we all laughed, even though it wasn't especially funny.

Uncle Albin went to get the street plan and we pored over it for a while, Paul's head just touching mine, while the grown-ups went into the kitchen and did the washing up.

That night my head was full of thoughts and it took me a long time to get to sleep. I had longed for change, yet now it felt as though everything was changing too fast. Paul wanted to get off the conveyor belt I was so keen to get on. Did I want to get on it without him?

When I finally slept, notions of change invaded my

dreams. The place was the same, but time had moved on. I no longer recognised the people around me, and yet somehow I was still myself, or some version of myself in a strange environment. It seemed to be a couple of centuries later and the invaders were no longer invaders, but overlords.

They're taking down the old church. Dressed timber is too valuable to waste, so they come in the night, carry away what they can. Each morning there is less of it and new dwellings are appearing at the other end of the village. I don't like what they're doing. That was a holy building and you just can't treat it like that. That's what I think, but I'm only a girl. I'm not made for thinking. My brother Elfgar says, anyway, they made some special prayers so it won't be holy any more. Then I ask him, 'What about the graves?'

'What about them?'

'All those people: our grandparents and great-grandparents, our forefather Aegfrith, the babies who died ... They were put in holy ground, with holy words, and now they haven't got the church there to keep watch over them.'

Elfgar growls at me, a sneer on his face. 'They're dead, Matilda.'

Since he married Wyfrun, he thinks he is superior to me and goes around with a knowing look on his face. He makes me angry, but I miss him sometimes. Being at home with the little ones is not the same without him there.

My mother thinks it is time I was married too. She says Brunloc's son has been asking for me. I don't want to be married. I've seen the hardships of my mother's life close up, and I don't want any of that. I do my share of the household tasks, watching the fire while the pot boils, spinning the long hairs that come from the sheep and untangling the threads on the great loom that stands near the doorway to catch the light. I am even learning the art of making loops of thread with a hooked bone needle, to make hats and stockings for my brothers and sisters. So far I have produced nothing that would fit even a doll.

All this I can do, and in time I will do more, but I know what else marriage means: every year my mother's belly swells and, in time, the new baby pushes out while she screams and bleeds. Each year it takes her longer to recover. My lord from the big house comes and inspects the baby. If it is a boy he says it is good that there will be another fine youth to work the land, and if it is a girl he says that is good, too, as she will produce more babies.

His way with the language is strange, but at least he talks our tongue. My grandmother remembers a time, she says, when they spoke only their own, and issued commands without words through the cudgel and the whip. It is better now, I think.

Paul took me to see the concrete cows the next morning. Although I had been prepared to dislike them, after all the teasing I'd had back home, they were lovely. They didn't look like real cows, but they were very cow-*like* in the way they stood around, grazing. I wasn't sure if they were white with black patches or black daubed with white. One of the smaller cows had been painted in stripes, as though wearing pyjamas, and another was wearing a hat and scarf. I wondered if they were the colours of a local football team, but Paul said they didn't have one yet. Apparently, the cows got 'decorated' like that all the time. Leaping astride the biggest cow, he started rolling around and lassoing the air rodeo-style. I was torn between laughing at the ridiculous spectacle he was making and telling him to get down in case someone came along to tell us off. That's how Dad had brought me up. Don't do things in case you get into trouble and, preferably, don't do things at all so that nothing bad can ever happen.

Looking at Paul – laughing and acting the fool even after the massive row with his parents – made me feel giddy inside. I wanted to be part of his world and jumped up behind him. The surface of the cow was so slippery I had to wrap my arms tightly round his waist. He didn't seem to mind and responded by laying his hand on my thigh. When we heard someone coming, we ran off and dived behind some bushes. And there, out of breath from laughing and running, Paul kissed me.

'Thanks, Mattie,' he said, touching my cheek lightly with his thumb. 'I'm so glad you're here.'

The rest of my time with Paul jumbles together in my memory. One afternoon we visited the Peace Pagoda, an unexpected structure glistening white and gold in the afternoon sun and seeming to speak of the numinous. One long lazy day we spent by the lake, the fearsome geese honking and running at us as if to say we were the intruders. I remember slipping on green slime at the water's edge and Paul buying me an ice cream because my new white shoes were ruined. We visited the Central Library, where a huge mural of the new town spanned two floors, freezing it in time, forever brand new. Outside, two girls, cast in bronze, whispered their secrets timelessly in a sculpture that is still there.

Milton Keynes fascinated me. There was glass and steel and rawness and newness, and there were the ancient villages that stood calmly as if to say: times come and times go and we have seen them all. I was learning more and more from my dreams and Paul's tuition. I felt certain that this sprawling place built on ancient foundations would one day fall into ruin, as the Normans' ambitious buildings had before them, as the Roman settlements had before them, as generation after generation takes possession of the land and holds it for a short time.

On my last day, Auntie Grace took me shopping for towels and sheets, the first that would be my very own and not chosen by my parents. I was so confident that I would soon be escaping the narrowness of my life at home in Liverpool that I was happy to buy things for uni even before my results came out. I should have known I was tempting fate.

'Will you two be all right on your own?' Auntie Grace asked, with a slightly worried expression as she and Albin headed out to dinner. 'I'm sorry, but we promised we'd go over and see the Jacksons before they move . . .'

'We'll be fine, Mum.' Paul's eyes had that wicked look again, and he was struggling to keep his jawline under control. Eventually it did widen into a grin. 'I'm sure we'll find something to do.'

Uncle Albin eyed the drinks cabinet. 'I expect you be sensible, Paul. Remember, Mattie's parents are trusting us we look after her . . .'

'Go on, enjoy yourselves. I'll look after Mattie, I promise.'

It wasn't the drinks cabinet that Uncle Albin should have been worrying about. We watched a film for a while and then Paul took my hand and led me gently upstairs. I was so nervous, a thousand butterflies in my stomach, but I don't think he'd done it before either and it was all a bit clumsy and over very quickly. I loved the sweet way he lay with me afterwards, stroking my collarbone with his fingertips, and the gentle little kisses he planted all the way down my face from my forehead to my chin.

Next morning, Paul was still asleep in his room as I got up and padded round the guest room doing the last of my packing and he was still asleep when

Auntie Grace announced that she was going to drive me home.

'It'll give me a chance to catch up with your mum,' she said brightly, but looking strained. I wondered if the plan was to leave Paul and Uncle Albin alone to thrash out Paul's future. He still hadn't appeared when Albin loaded my bags into the boot and hugged me goodbye. I looked up longingly at his window, still tightly curtained against the new day.

'Say goodbye to Paul for me, and tell him . . . thank him for me, for this week. For everything.' I left, feeling incomplete.

After I returned home, the church still haunted me. If I closed my eyes, I could see the sunlight slanting through the stained glass and settling in coloured pools on the floor; I could smell the ancient stone, feel the slight chill contrasting with the heat of the summer's day outside. In my mind's eye I could see, as though actually present, the pews, the medieval shields, the Jacobean coat of arms, the dusty piles of prayer books. In my dreams I was transported to the thirteenth century, watching the building continue, present in the lives of those who went before, myself and yet someone else, a woman of long ago.

*

The construction of the new church is far advanced and the walls are already above the height of a man. The chisels and hammers of the masons ring out from when the sun rises until it disappears below the horizon. I am sad that my grandmother will never see it. It is for her that I am named Matilda. She lived many years, but I wish that she was living still to see this new wonder in our village. She lies in her grave beside her own mother, near where the old church stood.

I crept from my bed early this morning. My husband stirred a moment and then was quiet again. It seems odd to me, still, to call him 'husband'. We were made man and wife but seven days ago, and I have hopes of bearing many children to work our portion of the land. After I had milked the goat and gathered fresh rushes, I walked over to the old wooden church at Broctone to pray for this boon to the Blessed Virgin. Father Edmund was saying Mass to a few of our neighbours, and I sat for a while, thinking of my grandmother and forgetting what I had come for.

When I came back, I stood with the village children awhile. They gather each day in a little group, open-mouthed with awe as the men sweat and struggle with the great stones. The skilled masons are starting to make a high stone arch that will one day form the boundary between the people and the holy things that only the priest may touch. When it is finished it will be above the height of two men. Watching them work is better entertainment than the May fair. Three days ago they made a scaffold of stout wooden poles, and clambered up, hauling a winding machine. We all cheered when the curved wooden frames were lifted slowly into place, while my kinsmen Martin and Sarles strained at the great turning handle on the machine at the very top of the scaffold. Today they have begun, slowly and with such great care, to raise up some of the shaped stones that will stay in place, perhaps for many years, even when the wooden framework is taken away.

Paul never knew about the baby. At first I didn't know, either. I wasn't sure really – I was so naïve – and so we continued to call each other, write silly notes, dream . . . Paul even came up to Liverpool to stay. I tried to show him around the same way he had entertained me in Milton Keynes, but I didn't know that many places and in the end he bought a map and had to show me around instead. My parents' anxiety was palpable every time we left the house, and we were constrained, uncomfortable with each other. The sense of fun and freedom had gone.

I felt miserable and that the whole visit had been a mistake, but on the very last day we took the bus to the Pier Head, and wandered along the landing stage, craning our heads to see the great winged birds atop the Liver Building, the golden sailing ship turning in the wind on the slender spire of the parish church.

'So, are we going to take a "Ferry 'Cross the Mersey" then?'

'Do you want to?' I was surprised. I didn't think he would be up for something like that.

Paul inhaled deeply. 'This smells a bit different to Milton Keynes!'

It was the raw, earthy, salty smell of my childhood. The slippery weed, darkly green, clung to the wooden posts left by the receding tide. Gulls screeched high above, descending every now and then to fight over discarded sandwiches and other careless scraps. I thought of how much more peaceful Paul's childhood must have been and wished we had been better friends then.

'Well?'

'OK, but I haven't been on one of these in years: we'd better look at the timetable.' I was suddenly nervous and the print swam in front of me, but we found what we needed to know and joined the queue for tickets.

A slight altercation broke out between some football supporters, blue scarves against red. It was a surprise – a really good one – when Paul put his arm protectively around me. I had missed our sense of closeness during the week. Then the ferry arrived. It shocked the wooden landing stage and I looked forwards to see the bow strike and bounce off the huge rubber tyres a few times before the crew could haul in the ropes and steady the vessel.

'Let them off first!' came the shout, but the last passenger was barely on dry land before we ran like children to be first on the upper deck and get the best seats. We laughed ourselves silly and that's what I will always remember of that day: the laughter. I hear it inside myself, even now, after so many years have passed.

We didn't disembark on the Wallasey side and instead pressed ourselves into a corner as everyone else shuffled down the gangplank. I think the first oncoming passengers were a bit startled to see us waiting there, but no one said anything and we were able to ride back to the Liverpool side, staying bold as brass in our seats.

I lost count of the times we crossed and recrossed the Mersey that afternoon. We talked non-stop: should or shouldn't Paul bow to his parents' wishes? If he didn't go to uni what would he do instead? Could he get away with working at some dead-end job while he thought about it? Or should he leave home and go travelling? We talked about my problems with my parents and a whole lot of other random stuff. For that one afternoon we were back on our old footing. By talking about the things that mattered, we were brought close again. As the wind tangled my hair, Paul kissed me for the first time that week and I felt alive and free.

And then it was mid-August, and the dreaded results were out. I waited for Paul to call me, because mine were good and it didn't seem fair to tell him I'd got my first choice until I knew how things stood with him. *Southampton here I come!* I wanted to shout, but I kept a lid on my excitement as I waited for the phone to ring, stalking the hall where it rested on a small table. When it finally did ring, I leapt at it so keenly that I managed to skin my knee on the wall. The first thing Paul heard was me going, 'Ouch!'

'Well that's a nice way to greet me!'

'Paul! I'm sorry – I just hurt my leg.' I paused. He didn't say anything. 'So how . . . how are you?'

'You'll never guess, never in a hundred years, never in a hundred, thousand million years...'

'Please tell me. I can't bear the suspense.'

'I got four As!'

My whoop of joy brought my dad running, with Mum not far behind, frowning.

'Paul got four As.'

I lost control of the phone after that. Mum wanted to speak to Auntie Grace, and then the phone got passed to Uncle Albin, and somewhere along the line Paul was being congratulated gruffly by my dad, and then they hung up.

So that was it. He'd got his place. He would be able to defer, which would keep Uncle Albin happy, and in the meantime he would spend a year travelling or working while he thought seriously about what he wanted. He would be able to come and see me in Southampton, too.

I still didn't know about the baby. I received a reading list and excitedly went to the bookshop to order the key texts. Mum started giving me lessons on how to iron and prepare my favourite meal. My hall of residence invited me over for an induction session, and Dad finally agreed that I could take the train. I told him he'd better get used to it.

*

I was all ready to go. My new, exciting life lay before me, full of promise and endless choices, but when term began, I was still at home, suffering the miseries of morning sickness. If my parents had tried to protect me before, now it was twice as bad. They veered between treating me as an invalid – ever so careful of my new fragility – and a naughty child, badgering me to tell them who the father was. They were convinced it was nothing to do with me, and I was convinced that if I told them the truth, Paul and his parents would suffer horribly for it. Mum and Auntie Grace had been friends for so long that I couldn't bear the thought of anything damaging their friendship.

But as the weeks passed I knew I'd have to tell Paul. I spent hours dreaming about us being together, reliving the summer in my mind. His year off would be a blessing: he'd be around to help me, get to know his child, ask me to marry him.

I finally plucked up the courage to phone him towards the end of October.

'No, love, he's no here.' Uncle Albin seemed surprised when I asked to speak to Paul. 'His term started weeks ago.'

'Oh.' Paul had changed his mind. He had gone to university without telling me. It felt like a betrayal.

'Anyway, how you getting on? Enjoying it?'

Mum and Dad hadn't told them. I mumbled something about everything being great and rang off.

'Who were you talking to, Mattie?' Mum never missed a trick. I lied and told her it was one of my school friends calling from her new halls.

A few weeks later I received a postcard from Paul.

Having a great time. The course is great. Thanks for persuading me to go.

Had I?

Then nothing until December: a card with the university crest on the envelope. He complained that he hadn't heard from me. He'd met a nice girl called Laura. He was bringing her home for Christmas and wondered if I'd like to meet her. I didn't reply.

Stella was born on 9 April 1988. The nurses were kind. They could see how alone I was, despite Mum and Dad being there throughout. The more they fussed, the more alone I felt. I tried not to think about Paul.

It had taken me a while to let Southampton know I wouldn't be taking up my place. It was hard to let go of my hopes.

Stella hardly slept for the first few months and I was so worried about her waking Mum and Dad in the next room that I tried to pick her up the moment she murmured. I was zombie-like with exhaustion. Then it was summer. I knew that I needed to make some decisions about my future, but all I could do was plod along, one foot in front of the other.

No one tells you how terrifying it is to have a child: not the having it, the stuff they explain at the antenatal classes. No, the really scary thing is how fragile a newborn baby is. 'Make sure to hold her head,' the midwife said. Only she didn't point out that if I didn't, my baby's tiny neck would snap. I held another human life in my hands, a life I could snuff out with one careless move.

Last year, Mum and Dad had tried to persuade me to apply to the local university, so I could live at home and wouldn't have to move away and live in some awful digs. Now, ironically, I was faced with being stuck at home with them forever. I had no money and no prospects. How could I study and get a job when I had a baby to look after?

In the end I started going to evening classes, really just to get out of the house. I was always the last to arrive. Stella was a slow feeder and took time to settle, so by the time I'd cleared up – Mum didn't like a mess in the kitchen – I was flustered and still had to gather my books and things. I registered for an extra A level, to be done in one year. If I ever did manage to start a degree, I now knew I wanted to study history.

Then one day, in Paul's final year – it must have been at the start of the summer term – the phone rang. I heard Mum's voice.

'Grace! How lovely to ... Oh my God! Oh my God!'

I flew down the stairs. Mum was sheet-white. She was listening intently, nodding, opening and closing her mouth. No sound was coming out.

'What? What?' I knew something terrible had happened. I just didn't know how terrible at that moment.

She motioned me to wait. I waited. Eventually she put the phone down and turned to me. She was shaking.

'Paul contracted meningitis, just before his exams. He died in hospital this morning.'

The funeral was held in All Saints, the church we'd explored that sunny morning when we were both eighteen. Paul never finished his history degree and I hadn't started mine and thought I never would. And Paul never knew about his child.

I watched the coffin being carried up the long path, gravel crunching beneath the well-polished shoes of the undertaker's men. We followed behind, silent, locked in our own thoughts. Everyone stood as it was carried in, and I could see they were all thinking the same thing: how could someone who had been so full of life be contained in that tight wooden box?

My parents had drifted apart from Grace and Abin since I'd had Stella. Nothing was ever said, but they hadn't called each other much and there had been no visit since Paul's that summer of our results. But grief had reunited our parents. Mum and Dad must have remembered how Grace and Albin had stood along-side them in their own loss as they stood together now in the pews reserved for family. Auntie Grace's head rested on my mum's shoulder.

I had left Stella at home with a friend, one of the mums I had met through toddler group. Her name – her very existence – was never mentioned. Would it have helped then, for Albin and Grace to know they had a grandchild?

The church was full of Paul's student friends, many

openly weeping. I wondered which tear-stained face belonged to Laura.

This place must have seen so much life and death in its seven hundred years. I sensed the trace left by all the other mourners from centuries past: my inward eye swept back through an immense procession of styles and fashions, people all so different in appearance and yet all so alike in their humanity. The human eye weeps now as it did centuries ago; the human body bends in grief and contorts in pain, for us just as it did for the people who first built the church.

I glanced at the grim, dark portrait of Lewis Atterbury, sometime rector of this parish, and remembered how Paul had told me the story of his drowning in Broughton Brook. There was the font from which Paul had been sprinkled with holy water as he started out on life's journey, and there, on the walls, memorials to those who had reached the end of theirs, at around the same age and just as suddenly, in corners of a foreign field in the dark days of World War One. Plaques and crosses bore witness to parents grieving, just as Grace and Albin were grieving now.

We followed the coffin out into the churchyard and stopped beneath the trees where I had once stood waiting for Paul to fetch the key. I was shocked to see how deep the hole was and wondered how long it had taken to dig. Then the vicar began the committal:

We have but a short time to live.
Like a flower we blossom and then wither:
like a shadow we flee and never stay.
In the midst of life we are in death;
to whom can we turn,
but to you, Lord, justly angered by our sins?

Was God angered by our sin, by Paul's and mine that evening? Was it even a sin, to love as innocently, as briefly, as we did then? Could the creation of new life really be a thing to be wished away?

The night after the funeral we stayed with Grace and Albin in their house in Broughton where they had welcomed me when I was so full of hopes for the future. I was glad Stella was with my friend, even though I missed her terribly. It wouldn't have been right to bring her here, for this.

The next morning I got up early, retracing my steps to the churchyard in the place I still thought of as Mideltone, to say my own private goodbye to Paul. The grass was damp on my sandalled feet, and

I took my time, edging carefully around the graves. There were several new ones since that earlier visit, in another lifetime. Some were tiny, their headstones carved with teddy bears and balloons. It made me sad that Claire had nothing like that. Making my way right round the church, I came at last into the shadow of the yew trees that had so frightened me. I looked down on the mound of earth that was all that was left to remind me that Paul had once been alive.

That's when I realised that I had to get my life sorted out. I owed it to Paul. And I owed it to our child.

When I returned to the house, I told Grace and Albin about Stella.

As in my life, so in my dreams, history had moved on. It was now a terrible time, a time of famine and plague. My grief for Paul and my fears for my own child mingled with those of a mother of long ago. She was connected with all those other Matildas, all those other Matties who had lived and died in this place.

My eyes are swollen with weeping. They will not let me near them, my little ones, not even for one last embrace before they are thrown into the pit. I will take the sickness myself, they tell me. I too will have the open sores, the fever, the same agonising death. What do I care for that, when my little ones are gone?

Last year I thought myself doleful enough for ten lives when my beloved Fulk passed beyond. That was not the sickness: his poor body was just worn through, like an old pair of shoes. We had battled the years of poor harvests, the land too sodden in the spring to turn with the plough, the seed rotting where it lay. We grew accustomed to the gnawing hunger in the belly, though I was never reconciled to a child starving at my breast when no milk came. Three babies I lost that way. But this last was different, so much more cruel, as if Satan himself stalked the land, seeking out those least able to stand against him. One day they were at Mass with me, running up the path and playing tag as they went; the next they were crying with thirst, their young skin breaking into weals.

I cannot bear to remember more. Father Peter blessed them in that church with holy water when they were but tiny babes. He made the sign of Blessed Jesu on their foreheads, and we rejoiced, Fulk and I, for each one of them. But they are denied the rites of Holy Mother Church in their untimely death; their pitiful little bodies must be taken far from hence, must be tipped in with scant ceremony and only the feeble prayers of their desolate mother to commend them to their maker. So many have died these past months; they lie with their play companions. I will take what comfort I may from that.

My Lord of Aylesbury's men are once more at work on the church. It was a good stout building of strong stone before, but small, and my lord wishes to spend good gold in making it bigger and finer. There are new ideas about building, the masons say, as they carve the stone around the windows until it looks like the ferns that grow in our woods. The old arch is too plain, they say, and must be embellished. I cannot think God cares overmuch for fancy decoration. Father Peter says God cares for the poor, though we see little show of it. I do not think my Lord of Aylesbury cares for the poor, even while he claims to honour God with all this building. What I think is that it is a pity he didn't expend his largesse on his tenants when we were near starvation. But that is ever the way of this world.

Fulk lies buried behind the church. I shall be stirred to anger if those men with their great feet disturb him as they work.

It had been really hard at first, studying for that extra A level, but the day I got my result – an A – I knew it had been worth it. The university admissions officer was helpful on the phone, and when I went to see him, dressed in my dark funeral skirt and blouse – the only respectable clothes I possessed, he made me an unconditional offer there and then.

Three years after I had expected to begin an English degree at Southampton, I embarked on a history degree in Liverpool. Dad managed to fit a desk and bookcase in my room and he and Mum made a sweet little bedroom for Stella next door. She was doing five mornings at playgroup by then, which made it all a bit easier, and on the days I had lectures, Mum collected her. Mum hadn't worked since before I was born and in truth had probably been at a bit of a loose end as I grew older. I think she was happy to find a role again.

Some days, I took Stella myself but I always felt like the odd one out. When the other mums dropped their kids off, they seemed to enjoy standing around for a gossip or going to get a coffee. I couldn't afford the time for any of that.

Usually, I tried to put in an hour or two of study after Stella was in bed. The house was quiet then, and at least Stella slept well once she did fall asleep. But then morning always seemed to come too soon, and as I hauled her into bed with me, hoping against hope that she would go back to sleep, which I don't think she did more than a couple of times in four years, well, those were the moments given over to sadness, when I tried to imagine having Paul with me to share some of the load.

What would he have thought of his daughter? She looked a bit like him, with her deep, dark eyes and knowing smile. What would he have done if I'd contacted him, let him know about our baby? Sometimes I imagined how he might have given up his course and rushed straight up to Liverpool to say: 'Wow – bullseye! Let's get married.' I imagined his smile and in my semi-dreaming state I could almost feel his hand stroking my arm and his face nuzzling my neck. Then reality would take over in the form of two little knees digging into my back and a hand tugging my hair. Stella's little voice: 'Go downstairs, Mummy?'

My first-year results were good. I passed with a merit. All those late nights, the running around and never feeling that I was on top of things at home or university – it was all worth the effort. I had proved that being a mother didn't mean the end of all my ambitions.

High on that achievement and my newly recovered confidence, I made a decision. I was a grown-up now. My life was back on track and it was time I stood on my own two feet. I would move out. All I had to do now was break it to my parents. What I hadn't expected was that they would have something to break to me first.

'Mattie, you've done well, really well. We're proud of you.'

I didn't like the sound of that. I was waiting for the 'but'.

'The thing is...'

Here it came.

'The thing is, your mother and I have been thinking. We've seen how hard the last year has been, balancing working at your studies and looking after Stella...'

'I couldn't have done it without you and Mum. You've been great. I owe you everything.'

'But how much longer do you seriously think you can keep this up? Another two years at university? Isn't it time to stop and focus on Stella?'

I had that terrible feeling again, the one I'd had when I was a teenager and they had asked me to apply to local universities. They didn't what me to grow up, to move on.

'You want me to give up? Now? After all my hard work?'

'Think about it, Mattie. It's not that we mind looking after Stella – although your mum's not getting any younger. But it's you. You're missing out. She's such a lively little thing. There's something new every day and you're not there to see it.'

My eyes filled with tears. Of course I wanted to be there to enjoy every moment with my little girl, every smile and every new word. But I also wanted to give her a better life. I wanted to fulfil my own dreams. And they wanted to narrow my horizons. I tried in vain to explain about the house-share and the nursery that had just opened up at the university. But they countered with questions about shared bathrooms and how Stella would sleep in a house filled with noisy students. They'd heard all about these student parties! It was clear that if I moved out, they would no longer support me. I would be truly on my own.

In the end, it was decided Stella and I would spend a few weeks of the summer vacation with Grace and Albin. Dad had bought me a little car and paid for driving lessons so I could transport Stella around more easily and I was truly grateful for this small measure of independence.

Reversing the journey Paul had made when he came to collect me in the summer of '87, we arrived at Auntie Grace and Uncle Albin's house and were welcomed with tea and cake.

I awoke next morning to find Stella already downstairs, being fed creamy scrambled egg by Auntie Grace. She didn't seem all that interested to see me. I asked Auntie Grace if she would mind looking after her while I went for a walk.

I tried to retrace the route I had once taken with Paul – unsure whether I was attempting to raise ghosts or lay them to rest – but so much seemed to have changed in the years since my first visit and even since the day after Paul's funeral when I set off to the churchyard on foot. After only a few minutes, I found myself brought up short by the realisation that I was no longer sure of the road. Where once their house had looked onto open countryside and farmland, now a crop of newly built houses stood fresh and proud, the diggers and piles of bricks witness to their recent construction. A skeletal roof truss arrived on a growling lorry as I turned the corner. This road should have led me to Milton Keynes Village, but I was confronted with a giant dual carriageway cutting right across my path. Surely, I thought, there was once a meandering country lane here, thick with glossy green growth and wild roses? I seemed to be in some sort of alternate universe: the same blue sky covered me, the same birdsong, and, starting to rise higher in the sky, the same golden sun: everything was the same but different.

Taking my life in my hands, I darted across the road, pausing on the central section to wonder whether I might orphan Stella in the process. I felt so sad: how could two villages that had been linked by a single road for hundreds of years now be severed by the planners of the new town?

By luck – or something more mysterious – I found my way to All Saints Church, passing through what seemed to be building works. Two diggers were motionless at one side of the site, like sentinels standing guard, while a group of men in high-vis jackets waited for their foreman to talk to a man in a suit and a hard hat. There were a few bystanders not far from where I had come on to the scene.

'Do you know what's going on?' I asked.

'They're working on the foundations for a car park – for the new pavilion.' The man jerked his head in the direction of some further earthworks.

'Not much happening!' I risked a smile.

'No. I don't think the boss is any too pleased about it, but once they found bones they had to stop.'

'Bones?'

'Human remains, looks like.'

Had I stumbled onto the site of a grisly murder? I watched as the conversation between the 'boss' and the suited man became more animated.

'Well, there's nothing I can do about it. The site will have to be closed down until further notice,' the latter was saying.

The foreman turned on his heel and issued some terse orders to the workers, who started to immobilise the diggers before climbing into their van and driving off. The wheels churned through the soft, clayey mud, flinging up clods seemingly in disgust at having to make a quick exit.

'Don't worry,' said my fellow bystander. 'This isn't a crime scene! The chap there is the borough archaeologist. Those bones are probably a few hundred years old. He's going to bring in a team, see what else they can find.'

The following week Auntie Grace showed me a cutting from the local *Citizen*: the bones were those of Saxons who had lived – and died – in the village a thousand years or more before. It seemed almost certain that it was a Christian burial ground, lending support to the view that there had been an earlier church there. A shiver went down my spine when I read that. I remembered the strong sense of a presence I'd experienced when I visited with Paul, as though time had looped back on itself and brought together those whose paths should never have crossed.

So the people of the middle ton had been there all the time, while the new village had grown around them. The houses had been built of wood and then brick, a splendid new church had been built, a wall enclosing it, and a new graveyard had taken their dead. Slowly the years had covered up the humble graves of the past and every trace of the people who had once been there was lost.

And now the new town was closing in on the old village. Every day it crept closer, as more people came and the Swan Pub, under its ancient thatch, buzzed with new voices, new accents. Milton Keynes Village had always been a place of change, and so, I realised, it would continue.

On our last morning, Stella was deep into the collection of Duplo that Grace and Albin had acquired ahead of our visit. They brought some of Paul's old toys out of the loft, but there was nothing there quite suitable for a toddler.

'You should have some of his things for her . . . for when she's old enough to hear about her father.' Grace's voice trembled and I know mine did too.

'I'd like that. Do you have any photographs?'

Another box was hauled down: old exercise books, the writing growing bolder and more assured, the spelling mistakes fewer as the years passed. And another with photos of Paul in his school uniform on his first day at school; on holiday with his parents; at scout camp with muddy knees, carrying a pile of sticks. There was a faded picture of us as children, half-turned away from each other and looking grumpy. We had been taken to the seaside while they were staying with us in Liverpool and I don't think either of us enjoyed it. I remember finding Paul tiresome and I am sure he had done his best to wind me up. Maybe that's what having a sibling would have been like. There were no pictures of us when we were older.

Then it was back to Liverpool. I reached an understanding with Mum and Dad. I went back to uni but continued to live at home, while they cosseted Stella instead of me.

For two years nothing changed externally, save my daughter's height marks on the door frame and my parents' grey hairs. Inside though, my conviction grew that it was time to respond to that mysterious sense of being part of something infinitely bigger than myself that I had first felt beneath the trees in the churchyard.

About three years later I happened to visit Grace and Albin on my own. I was by then partway through my theological training and feeling much more secure. Stella was growing up fast. She had started at the school down the road from Mum and Dad and I was happy to leave her with them for a few days.

After I'd had a cup of tea with Grace and Albin, I set out to visit the church. I parked my car in what was now a properly maintained car park and was surprised to find a number of cars already there. I had assumed it would be deserted on a Thursday afternoon in November. But I thought nothing more of it as I headed towards the churchyard, wanting to spend a few minutes at Paul's grave telling him how Stella was getting on and what I was doing with my own life.

The arrival of a sleek black hearse interrupted

my plan. I tried to remove myself discreetly from the scene, but found my way blocked by a group of people heading in my direction down the gravel path. The vicar, in black cassock and heavy black cloak, moved towards me, holding out a sheet of paper.

'Welcome!'

It was disconcerting; his manner didn't seem right for a funeral and no one was dressed in black. I started to mumble about not knowing the deceased, but he stopped me.

'No, none of us did. They died a very long time ago!'

He smiled and explained that, because the bones had to be moved, they had decided it was only right that they should have a proper Christian burial.

'We believe there are the remains of a hundred Saxon people in there.'

The dark-suited men had now brought out two wooden coffins. They were staggering under the weight: no surprise, if each coffin contained the bones of fifty individuals.

'Do stay, if you are able,' the vicar smiled. 'They don't have anyone else to see them off, only us.'

The coffins had been brought inside the gate and laid side by side on the grass. It was only then that

I noticed the deep hole that had been dug alongside the path. I remembered the hole that Paul's coffin had disappeared into and how final it had seemed. And now these unnamed, unknown people, his ancestors, perhaps, had claimed our pity and reminded us of our common humanity.

The burial service proceeded in an abbreviated form, and as the words were spoken, and the coffins lowered, I thought how many years make up a life and how Stella and I had only really begun ours.

Milton Keynes Village, 2012

I CLEAR AWAY the breakfast things and soak in the bath for a while, still full of old thoughts. The hot tap is dripping, and I think absent-mindedly that I must see about having it fixed. I climb out stiffly and luxuriate in the new bath sheet I bought as I prepared to move to my new home.

Opening the wardrobe, I find that I do not know how to dress for today. In the early days of motherhood it was easy. I picked the least creased item from the ironing pile, checked for stains, sniffed it and put it on. For a while I hardly brushed my hair before looping it into an elastic band. But now I must choose my clothes by the message they will convey. I remember how strange it felt, the first time I put on clerical dress, but satisfying too, especially as the road had been a long one. My parents and Grace and Albin helped, each taking their turn to have Stella during my residential weekends and placements. There was, I think, a small measure of healing in that for everyone.

Stella is a little girl no longer: twenty-four last birthday and off on her travels again. A gap year, university: the moment she left school she claimed her independence. I have tried to give her the freedom I never had, although I am better placed now to understand my parents' anxieties. I can barely imagine what it was like when their little girl didn't come back.

I have loved all the parishes in which I have served. It was a privilege to stand at the altar of churches brand new and ancient, in housing estates and pretty villages, half full and bursting at the seams, traditional and achingly forward-looking. Stella coped pretty well with being a clergy child, especially one without a father. And now I am here, back where it all began, in this place, with its memories . . .

The village is fast being swallowed up by the new town. The locals call it a city. *Welcome to the New City and Borough of Milton Keynes*: the board reads as you drive in. Maybe next year will be the one when its official city status is announced.

When the planners first came, they were determined to build something different from all the other new towns, a glorious place of low-rise, low-density buildings and endless green spaces. There would be no traffic jams, no traffic lights: roundabouts would keep order. Communities would form naturally within the grid squares. It used to be said that there are more trees than people in Milton Keynes, and I believe it, even now, with the town still growing each year.

But when they mapped their plans onto the existing landscape, they couldn't erase what was already there, what had been there for two thousand years, and so the settlements from before the time of William's Domesday Book remained in situ, punctuating the new town, the past co-existing with the present. I had felt the past all around me from my earliest visit, as though it was telling me something about the nature of our very existence. We are not so different from those people of long ago.

Even in Auntie Grace's Broughton, there is change: Broughton Brook has been rerouted, although in winter it is quite full, and on a dark night I can imagine the Revd Lewis Atterbury riding home towards warmth and a dry bed only to fall into its dark waters. The new bridge has great steel suspension wires and, rather comically, a light on top, as if to warn very low-flying aircraft.

At the centre of Milton Keynes Village are still

the village green and the pub, thankfully rebuilt after burning down one Christmas when someone put too many logs on the fire and the thatch caught alight. With a wonderful acknowledgement of Shakespeare's 'whirligig of time', the grid square in which it stands is now named Middleton. I cried when I learned that: I so wished Paul could have known.

The church still stands, as it has for seven hundred years, solid and watchful, at the heart of this community. Near the gate is a slate slab marked with a Saxon cross. Beneath it lie the bones of the Saxons who lived and died in this place and who would have been astonished to see what it has become. Alongside the cross the slate is carved with these words from the prophet Ezekiel:

> *He asked me: son of man, can these bones live?*
> *I said: O Sovereign Lord, you alone know.*
> *Ezekiel 37.3*

As vicar here, I will be able to pay my respects each time I come to the church. I will also be able to pay my respects to another grave, further around, near the dark yew trees. I wonder what Paul would say if he could see me now, and whether he would be astonished to see what I have become.

Inside the church is a list of the priests who have cared for the people of this village over the years, who have listened to their troubles, chided their sins, visited their sick, buried their dead. Now I am to be one of them. When I leave this place my name will appear at the end of this list. It seems to me that there is really very little separation between the living and the dead.

And so the past and the present collide and are swallowed up in one another, and the day I cavorted in the churchyard with Paul and the day I wept at his grave, and today as I begin my new life, are all one, and the days and the lives of those whose bones lie beside the path are part of my life too.

HOMETOWN TALES

AVAILABLE NOW FROM W&N